abc Guide to Fit K

A companion for parents and families

Easy steps to family fitness and health in the age of obesity

Dr Phillip Mason, Katherine Swan and Adrian Stone

Contents

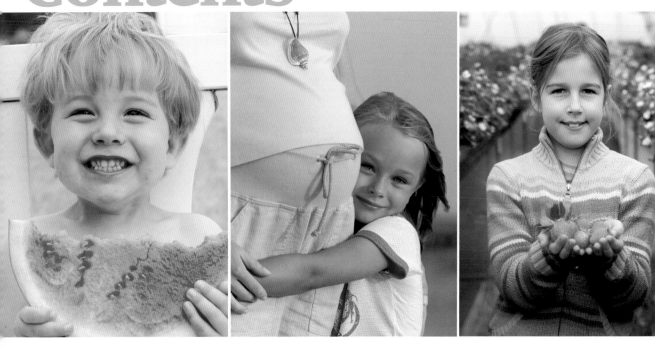

INTRODUCTION 4

GENERATION O 8
Why many of our children are becoming overweight
or obese

DIFFERENT STAGES FOR DIFFERENT AGES 14
Understanding your child's needs is important

FOOD FOR THOUGHT 28
Understanding and solving weight problems

FOOD MONSTERS 38
Other common food-related problems

A PLATE FOR LIFE 48
The food basics: variety, smaller portion sizes,
eating less sugar and fat

BETTER BEVERAGES 64
Juggling water, milk, juices and soft drinks

MIND YOUR Ps AND Qs! 72
Understanding food marketing and labels

LIFE: BE IN IT 80
Understanding the importance of exercise and being
active

PARENTS AS ROLE MODELS 90
Encouraging better family health and wellbeing
begins at home

SLOW AND STEADY WINS THE RACE 98
Being consistent, taking time to rest and working
together

IT'S A WRAP! 104
Healthy recipes and cooking tips for the whole family

HELPFUL RESOURCES 124

INDEX 125

Introduction

As food becomes more plentiful in today's society, so does information about nutrition. Understandably many parents are intimidated and overwhelmed by the sheer amount of food choice and nutritional information available, given the constant stream of new products on supermarket shelves, and often contradictory messages from the media and self appointed experts telling parents what their children should eat or avoid, and how much exercise children should get. However confusing the messages, understanding basic nutrition and exercise has become increasingly more important as families face a growing list of health problems related to over-consumption, poor food choice, and lack of exercise.

Childhood obesity now occurs among school-aged children in Australia and the UK at a rate of about 20-25%, and other health concerns – such as attention deficit disorders, asthma, and cardiovascular problems – are also on the rise. Today's diet-related health problems have coincided with a decrease in food quality and an increase in food quantity. Families today are much busier than they were in the past, and the lack of time for food planning and preparation has made possible a whole new world of convenience foods and aggressive food marketing. Convenience foods frequently replace fresh ingredients and home-cooked meals, as evidenced by the fact that a large percentage of today's children eat a diet low in fresh fruits and vegetables. Unfortunately, convenience foods typically have little or no nutritional value, turning whole meals into a deluge of empty kilojoules.

Today the average person consumes almost 70 kg of sugar a year, up from less than 5 kg a year only a decade ago.

Regular activity and exercise, an aspect of healthy living that used to be much more prevalent in our children's lives, has also fallen to the hustle and bustle of modern society. Fear for our children's safety and a lack of time to spend supervising outdoor play have resulted in a trend toward less demanding activities for children, who spend more time each day watching TV than engaging in active play. Ironically, although parents may sponsor many sedentary activities out of concern for their children's safety, a lack of active play in childhood can set the stage for poor health and weight problems later in life.

Although society may indirectly influence your family's habits with hectic schedules, media hype – with its fad diets and food marketing – plays a more direct role in steering consumers away from healthy eating habits. Food manufacturers often choose to highlight one or two health benefits of their products, encouraging consumers to view each product as "a good source of vitamin C" or "a great source of calcium" – but really distracting the consumer

from the fact that the products have no other redeeming qualities, and are in fact loaded with sugar.

In relation to childhood obesity, the advertising and media hype surrounding the negative impact of fat and the benefits of low-fat or non-fat foods has been considerable. However consumers who do not read food labels properly, particularly the nutritional panel, do not realize that the manufacturers of these products more often than not compensate for the lack of fat by adding extra sugar – which results in just as many empty kilojoules (if not more) as the food contained in the first place. In fact, the media focus on fatty foods as the culprit and related decline in the consumption of fat in food has actually coincided with an increase in obesity and related health problems. As fat consumption has fallen, there has been a significant increase in the amount of sugar we eat.

Modern society also heavily markets an enormous variety of diets touting one method of eating over another, from low GI diets to miracle shakes and other weight loss programs. However dieting and fad diets are difficult to maintain and also encourage unhealthy dramatic fluctuations in weight – as the dieter quickly loses weight on a temporary eating regimen, and just as quickly rebounds and gains it back.

Finding A Better Way

Eating better and exercising more can help you and your family shed not only the excess weight, but also the health risks that came with your old lifestyle. The risk of cardiovascular problems is decreased; childhood diseases such as attention disorders and asthma can be more easily controlled; and even your energy levels will benefit.

A family effort is one of the most important factors in changing your family's lifestyle. It is important for the entire family to know and understand the reasons for the changes, and the best way to do this is to involve everyone in the entire process, from start to finish. Involving the entire family in planning meals, grocery shopping, and food preparation not only lightens your workload, but also allows everyone to have fun and experiment. Family activities are also important, as they ensure that children can be supervised and stay active at the same time, as well as motivating everyone with some good old-fashioned fun.

Eliminating unhealthy foods from your family's diet may seem like the most challenging part, but it needn't be painful. Fad diets frequently fail because they focus on dropping the weight quickly, and therefore must enforce a strict diet from day one. When you are making the change to a healthier lifestyle, however, you can focus more on longevity than immediate results, and will therefore be able to take your time. Eliminating problem foods and introducing healthy alternatives can be done in small, manageable bites, allowing the entire family to adjust to the changes before introducing others.

Despite the fact that many of these habits will require you to resist the pull of modern society – as you try to find time to prepare meals or exercise together, for instance, or as you eliminate junk foods from your family's diet – you will find that society's conveniences can sometimes help your cause. For instance, the availability and competitiveness of modern grocery stores provides a vast selection of fresh, natural, and organic foods. Many grocery stores keep late hours, allowing you to shop when it is most convenient for you. Also, between parks and gyms, dance classes and sports teams, there is a wide variety of exercise for you and your family to choose from, ensuring that everyone will be able to find at least one activity that they like to do.

It's true that children's diets have changed fundamentally in recent decades and that these changes are having a significant impact on their wellbeing. However, don't think that because certain health risks have risen for our children compared to previous generations that our parents and grandparents understood more about carbohydrates, protein, and nutrient-rich foods than we do. The truth is, they knew less about the science of nutrition, yet they understood the importance of balanced meals and food variety to sustain their family. They also understood the benefits of exercise and active play. It's this knowledge, together with tools to help you decipher modern food choices and lose weight that is the simple message of this book.

Despite your busy schedules, the push for food advertising, and the power of the media, better health is within your family's reach. The following chapters will help you understand and implement a healthy diet and active lifestyle that will benefit your entire family, now as well as in the long run.

1

Generation O

Why many of our children are becoming overweight or obese

Quick Chapter Guide

- ✔ Understanding the causes of weight problems and obesity in children
- ✔ Convenience foods and television: a double-edged sword
- ✔ Changes in the way children socialize: the decline of active play
- ✔ How does obesity affect my child's health?
- ✔ The importance of a family effort to foster change
- ✔ Keys to emphasizing healthy habits at home

Generation O

Why our children are becoming overweight and obese

It's clear that weight problems are affecting more of our kids than ever before. In the last decade the number of overweight children in the UK, US and Australia has almost doubled. Weight problems can be difficult to come to terms with for both parents and children. The first step to making positive changes is to understand why childhood obesity occurs and the impact it can have on your child's health. The next step is to help kids moderate poor food choices and be more active by teaching healthy habits that they will retain for the rest of their lives.

As daunting as the task may seem, all it truly takes is a series of small changes in lifestyle. Children and adults alike will benefit from better food choices, and regular activity, whether overweight or not.

HOW DOES OBESITY IN CHILDREN HAPPEN?

Over the years, fad diets have blamed just about every part of food consumption for weight gain - excess kilojoules, fat, carbohydrates, and so on. This has created many misconceptions regarding proper nutrition, all of which must be corrected before the problem of obesity can be addressed. Unless there is an underlying medical reason, most weight problems emerge when an individual takes in more kilojoules (energy) from food than he or she uses. The body stores the unnecessary energy as fat, to be used at a future date; however, if the individual continues to take in more energy than needed, the body will continue storing the excess as fat. If continued, over time this cycle of overeating results in the individual becoming overweight – and, eventually, obese.

WHY ARE CHILDREN BECOMING OVERWEIGHT AND OBESE?

Poor nutritional choices: The convenience toll
Kids these days eat differently than previous generations, and the values of modern society have meant that more energy-dense, nutrient-poor foods are available to children on a daily basis. Aside from the convenience foods they consume, children and teens are subjected to relentless junk food advertising. Sugary foods, especially soft drink and fruit juice, pose a serious problem: in 2001, a study showed that simply drinking soft drink regularly caused a 60% increase in a child's chances of becoming obese. The consumption of soft drinks continues to rise annually, with the average Australian child drinking in excess of 110 litres per year. In the UK and US, the situation is even worse, with the average child consuming more than 200 litres of soft drink per year. Fast foods like pizza, hamburgers, potato chips, chocolates and other convenience foods have also enjoyed a steep rise in consumption. Conversely, the popularity of fresh fruit and vegetables has declined.

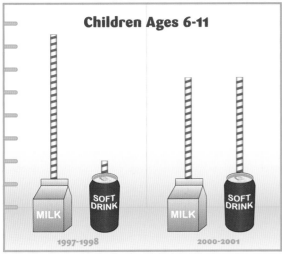

Generation O Kids Prefer Soft Drink to Milk

Children Ages 6-11

500ml

MILK | SOFT DRINK | MILK | SOFT DRINK

1997-1998   2000-2001

0ml
Average
Daily
Intake

*In 1978 US children aged 6-11 drank about 4 times as much milk as soft drink. In 2002 they drank about the same amounts of milk and soft drink. Given recent consumption rates it is likely that the next generation of children will drink more soft drink than milk. In addition to increased risk of obesity - accelerated tooth decay and bodily nutrient loss are also linked to soft drink intake.

"In 2001, a study showed that simply drinking soft drink regularly caused a 60% increase in a child's chances of becoming obese."

Children are less active than ever before

While children eat more junk food than ever before, they are also considerably less active than previous generations. Generation O's shift towards more sedentary pastimes has occurred for a number of different reasons:

Television: A double-edged sword: Modern society's fascination with television is a double-edged sword. On one side, it's a passive activity that displaces other activities, preventing kids from burning as much energy as they consume. On the other, you have the food advertising that children are continually bombarded with throughout their programs - urging them to eat more and more, even as they exercise less.

Food advertising is particularly dangerous because children tend not to understand its intent to persuade and manipulate. The same commercials are played relentlessly, until a child knows them by heart. Marketers essentially program children so they instantly recognize the products on grocery store shelves and make their demands.

Not surprisingly children who watch the most television tend to consume more energy-dense and nutrient-poor foods than other kids, and are the fattest.

Changes in children's play: The way kids play has also changed in recent years. Children's play has become more and more dependent on television, video games, and other sedentary forms of entertainment. This has been a result of several different influences in modern society including changes to our living and recreational environments, rising fears of injury or abduction, and the fact that many busy parents have less time to attend to their children's needs – including supervising outdoor recreation and play.

Changes to activity at school: The school system's attitude toward physical education has also changed over the years; whereas physical education used to be a regular part of children's curricula, budget cuts and other priorities have diminished the frequency of these classes considerably. Ironically, organized school sports have also become more competitive, alienating many children who previously would have participated for fun and social benefits, rather than any professional aspirations.

Changes in the ways children socialize: In addition to the role parents' busy schedules play in encouraging more indoor play and less outdoor activity, technology has also had a direct effect on children's social lives. With the advent of mobile phones and the Internet, children no longer have to seek out social settings. Rather than hanging out with friends, children can communicate with them via mobile phone or Internet instant messages. And instead of getting together for play dates, children can play games with each other over the Internet. Consequently, technology has turned socialization into more of a passive than an active pastime.

Other factors

In addition to poor food choices and less activity, studies have connected obesity to a variety of other factors. In some studies, it appears that children with a low birth weight are more likely to become obese in childhood, perhaps because of their bodies' overzealous attempts to try to catch up to normal development. Oddly enough, breastfeeding also seems to have an impact on childhood obesity, with a child's chances of obesity decreasing the longer they are breastfed as a baby. Other studies have shown a connection between the mother being overweight during pregnancy, and the child's likelihood of becoming obese. Although it's not clear whether it is due to genetics or environment, there is a clear link between parental obesity and childhood obesity.

There are many influences that seem to be linked with obesity in children, but one thing is quite clear: obese children are likely to become obese adults. Because of the severe impact obesity can have on one's health, the individual causes of childhood obesity should be considered very carefully, and family orientated efforts made to counter them wherever possible.

HOW DOES OBESITY AFFECT MY CHILD'S HEALTH?

Besides the self-esteem issues created by weight problems in childhood, obesity also carries with it a host of other health problems. Being overweight or obese greatly increases your child's risk of diabetes; joint injuries and arthritis; digestive problems; hormonal imbalances; and depression. If left untreated, childhood obesity can even cause cardiovascular problems, just as in adults. The longer the weight problem persists, the greater a child's chances of developing secondary health problems - and the more severe these problems may be.

Additionally, because the body is still developing, weight problems during childhood have a profound impact on an individual's weight later in life. While a child's body is developing, fat cells increase in number, according to their weight. However, in an adult's body, the number of fat cells is fixed - as the adult gains or loses weight, only the size of the fat cells can change. This means that individuals who were overweight as children tend to have trouble losing weight as adults because of the greater number of fat cells established during childhood. Unsurprisingly, studies show that as many as three-quarters of obese children remain obese throughout adulthood.

Importantly, the earlier you take action to reverse your child's weight problems, the better off he or she will be in the long run.

FACILITATING CHANGE: THE IMPORTANCE OF A FAMILY EFFORT

Finding a solution to childhood obesity doesn't have to mean major changes, but it does require that the changes made be a family effort. Otherwise, you're doing little more than putting your child on a diet – which is a temporary solution to a weight problem, and does nothing to instil lifelong healthy living habits in your child.

Making the solution into a family endeavor benefits your child in several ways:

- ✓ It enables you to make a more lasting impression on your child. By including your child in making grocery lists, planning meals, and planning activities, you are teaching him or her not only the importance of making healthy choices, but also how to make them.

- ✓ Just as the entire family can be involved in changing the family's eating habits, families can work together toward a healthier exercise regimen. Not only do family activities teach children that exercise can be fun, they also allow the children to be supervised, minimizing accidents and other problems.

- ✓ When changes are made as a family, you also have the opportunity to reinforce the lessons you are teaching your child by modelling the behaviour yourself. Children learn a great deal by watching and imitating role models.

- ✓ Focusing the entire family on the goal of living healthier lives enables you to produce a counterforce strong enough to resist the peer pressure and cultural influences your child faces outside of the family.

- ✓ Making the solution a family endeavor also means everyone will benefit, parents and children alike.

Making changes as an entire family is part of what makes the solution different than the temporary fix of putting your child on a diet. It is the family environment and values children take with them when they step outside the house and enter the world on their own that have the greatest impact.

THE BENEFITS OF A HEALTHY LIFESTYLE

Besides the obvious decrease in obesity-related health risks, making the change to a healthier lifestyle has many benefits for the entire family. Healthy children are happy children: they suffer from fewer self-esteem and anxiety problems, and they tend to be more involved in recreational activities. The adults in the family will also benefit from the change: a healthier lifestyle will counteract the effects of the sedentary jobs many adults hold, reducing depression and increasing energy levels and wellbeing.

2

Different Stages for Different Ages

Understanding your child's needs is important

Quick Chapter Guide

- ✔ Children's growth and development is divided into major stages from birth and preschool through to adolescence and teenage years
- ✔ Each stage is different, and has unique growth needs and challenges
- ✔ Understanding your child's development stage is critical in raising healthy happy children
- ✔ Parental guidance, flexible communication, good nutrition and plenty of age-appropriate activity are all important
- ✔ The importance of being caring, flexible, and attentive.

Different Stages for Different Ages

Understanding your child's needs is important

Good nutrition and exercise is important in childhood, not only to foster lifelong healthy habits, but also for supporting healthy development throughout these critical years. As children grow and change, so do their nutritional needs. In order to help children practice better nutrition and learn to make healthier lifestyle choices, parents need to know some basic facts about physical growth and emotional development during childhood and adolescence. Additionally, a child's social development in each stage can create unique challenges to the parents' goal of fostering healthy habits.

It's important to note that although each of the following developmental stages are sequential – meaning that a child has to attain one stage's level of development before moving on to the next – each child grows at his or her own unique pace. At any stage, however, if your child rapidly gains or loses weight, it may be necessary to consult with your family doctor.

BIRTH TO TWO YEARS

The first 2 years of a child's life are full of new experiences; babies grow so quickly that they may seem to change overnight. It's important to realize that their needs for nutrition and activity are changing just as fast as they are - you must adapt quickly to each new change, perhaps even anticipate the next, if you are to keep up with them.

Physical Growth and Development

Babies grow rapidly during their first year. To maintain this rate of growth and change, their bodies must have a constant stream of nutrients. For at least the first few months, breast milk or high-quality formula satisfies this need. Beginning at 4-6 months, your child will start requiring additional nutrients from solid foods.

After the first year, your baby's growth may slow noticeably. Since the foods children eat fuel their growth, they may reflect this change by having less of an appetite for a little while. To ensure infants and toddlers are getting everything they need from their diet, make meals and snacks as nutritious and energy-dense as possible. Importantly, don't hesitate to voice your concerns to your family doctor in any instances of poor weight gain.

Social and Emotional Development

All children – even babies and toddlers – are very curious. During the first 2 years, a child is getting to know their body and what it's capable of. From holding their head up for the first time and learning to crawl and walk, to trying new foods, your baby is driven by the urge to interact with and explore the world.

As babies approach a year old, their awareness of the people in their lives becomes more complex. They begin to realize the difference between their primary caregivers and other adults, and what it means. Around a year of age, therefore – give or take a few months – your baby may begin to exhibit separation anxiety, getting upset for the first time when Mum or Dad leaves them. Despite separation anxiety, however, toddlers continue to explore the world around them, confident and secure in their parents' presence.

As your child approaches 2 years of age, emerging independence may become a key issue, as they test you again and again. Temper tantrums and deliberate disobedience are only another form of exploration; however, they should be managed with firm boundaries, and consequences when they are broken.

Because emotional development is such a critical part of these early years, all of your interactions with your child should have a strong foundation of love and support. Frequent verbal and physical expressions of affection are vital to your child's sense of security and trust; while still remembering the importance of being mindful of expectations and boundaries.

Nutritional Requirements

During the first 4-6 months of your child's life, all of their nutritional needs are satisfied by breast milk or high-quality formula. If a choice is available, an infant should be breastfed, as nature's dietary plan is better for infants than even the best formula. Breast milk is naturally enriched with everything your infant needs for strong, healthy development. Breastfed infants also get sick less often than formula fed infants, and they have less of a chance of being overweight in childhood. It is recommended that your infant be breastfed for the first 6-12 months – the longer, the better.

When breastfeeding is not an option, select a formula that is enriched with iron and other nutrients, making it almost – if not quite – comparable to breast milk. Whether breastfed or formula fed, infants who don't get much sun exposure should be given a vitamin D supplement.

Starting at about 6 months of age, you can begin feeding your baby pureed or mashed solids in addition to milk. Start with iron-enriched baby cereals and other grains and move on to fresh vegetables and fruits. To start, offer 1-2 teaspoons of one new food at a time after a milk feed. Solids will teach your baby about eating and provide extra iron, protein and vitamins. Increase gradually to 1-2 tablespoons, 2-3 times a day. New foods can be added every couple of days. Try each new food separately in case your baby reacts to it. When offering a new food, watch for signs of an allergic reaction. If your child develops a rash, exhibits signs of swelling, has difficulty breathing, or vomits during or soon after eating a new food, call your doctor. Mashed pumpkin, potato, carrots, peas, banana, stewed apple or pear are good first choices.

Because it's never too early to start modelling good eating habits, babies and toddlers should be introduced to vegetables before fruits so they don't become accustomed to sweet foods first, and parents should refrain from adding salt, butter or sugar to meals.

Between 6-9 months – once babies begin to bite and chew – mashed, minced, diced and grated foods can be introduced, including meats, mashed beans and lentils, rice and pasta, egg and yoghurts. It's important to supervise your child while eating and be aware of any foods that may pose potential choking hazards.

There is no need to limit fat intake at this period of a child's development; in fact, since fat is needed for the continued development of your child's brain, foods such as full cream milk are recommended for children under 2 years. Nutrients such as calcium, iron, and vitamins A, C, and D are also important at this stage.

At this stage, children's appetites are fairly small, but their active little bodies quickly burn through the energy taken in at each meal. Therefore, babies and toddlers should be fed between 4-6 small, nutrient-rich meals or snacks each day.

Proper hydration is just as important for your baby or toddler as it is for an older child or an adult. As your baby starts eating more solid foods and depending less on breast milk or formula for nourishment, you will need to make sure to provide enough fluids, particularly water. Keeping a colourful sipper cup filled with water and easily accessible to your child is a good way to encourage proper hydration.

Activity Requirements

Babies and toddlers need room to explore their bodies and what they are capable of. When your child is an infant, this may simply mean providing plenty of time on the floor, both on the stomach and the back, surrounded by colourful, interesting toys. This allows babies to practice grasping, lifting their heads, and eventually rolling and crawling. Before long, however, your child will learn to walk and run, and you'll need to allow sufficient space for exploring new skills.

Family activities can begin during this stage – the earlier, the better. Playing with Mum and Dad will encourage your child to hone new-found skills, not to mention make the entire experience more enjoyable for everyone.

Although children in this stage enjoy lots of activity, they also tire quickly from the physical exertion. As a result, they may take more frequent, but shorter, naps, effectively sabotaging any ideas you might have had of a strict nap schedule. Because of the new demands on your child's body, it's advisable to allow them to nap when they are tired, just as you feed your child when they are hungry.

Common Problems and Other Needs

Carefully monitoring your children's health and wellbeing is important; below are some examples of other common issues for infants and toddlers:

- ✓ **Poor weight gain** – Sometimes children do not gain weight properly, either for medical reasons or because their diet is not sufficient. Children have very small appetites; to ensure that your children are getting everything they need from their diet, make their meals and snacks as nutritious and energy-dense as possible. Also, don't hesitate to voice your concerns to your family doctor, who will check your child for any medical reasons for the poor weight gain.

✔ **Teething** – Between 4-7 months of age, your baby's first tooth will begin pushing through the gums; each of your baby's 20 baby teeth will emerge during the next couple of years. Teething may cause drooling, sore gums, low fever, and irritability. If your baby seems distressed, refrigerated teething rings may relieve some of the discomfort; however, if your baby exhibits severe distress, or physical symptoms such as a high fever and diarrhoea, you should call your doctor.

✔ **SIDS** – Sudden Infant Death Syndrome is the number one cause of death in infants. Although SIDS is relatively unpredictable, there are a few simple precautions you can take to protect your baby. For example, simply putting infants to sleep on their backs has been shown to reduce the number of SIDS deaths by more than 40%. Breastfeeding, dummy use, and firm bedding with only a light blanket are also linked to a reduced risk of SIDS.

Visit www.sidsandkids.org for more information.

QUICK TIPS FOR PARENTS

✔ Breastfeeding your infant for the first 6-12 months promotes healthy development, strengthens the immune system, and reduces the risk of childhood obesity. Start introducing mashed or pureed solids at about 6 months.

✔ Provide a variety of foods from all food groups.

✔ Offer 4-6 smaller meals or snacks each day.

✔ Provide opportunities for your child to explore and practice their physical abilities.

✔ Allow for frequent naps.

✔ Be mindful of other needs, especially for infants, who can be especially sensitive to changes in their environments.

2 TO 5 YEARS

Your child's preschool years are an exciting time. During this stage, they are growing quickly, both physically and mentally. Your child's physical abilities may surprise and delight you, and many parents enjoy their preschooler's blossoming cognitive and language skills. Because of their developing awareness, this stage is an ideal time to start reinforcing healthy nutrition, exercise, and decision-making.

Physical Growth and Development

Between 2-5 years of age, your child's body is not growing as quickly as it did in infancy, but it still needs to be properly fueled for plenty of development and activity. Children during this stage tend to settle into a regular napping schedule of one 2-3 hour nap per day; some children may grow out of naptime altogether. However,

your child is learning many new gross and fine motor skills, and will need sufficient rest in order to practice them. Naptime should not be discarded unless your child shows clear signs that it is no longer necessary, such as being able to skip a nap without getting cranky in the evening.

Social and Emotional Development

It is during the preschool years that children begin to grasp social concepts such as friendship. Although they begin to favour playing with other children as opposed to playing alone, they also tend to exhibit rigid gender typing: for example, boys roughhouse or play trucks with other boys, and girls play dolls or house with other girls.

Along with their developing social skills, preschool children are also learning to recognize and communicate their feelings. Your preschooler will often tell you when they are happy, angry, or sad. They will also demonstrate a push for independence. Clear boundaries and appropriate consequences for crossing them are important; however - as with children of any age - preschoolers need plenty of love, encouragement, and support from their parents.

Nutritional Requirements

As noted, children tend to continue their quest for independence during this stage. It's normal for mealtime to be affected. Even though your child may start rejecting foods they have eaten before, try not to become discouraged. Instead, remain positive and continue to offer your child a variety of healthy food choices. However, you should place limits on how much choice you offer your child - if you ask your child, "What do you want for dinner?" they are likely to choose their favourite food every time. Instead, offer to prepare several different choices and let them decide.

If your child exhibits a pattern of refusing a certain food, they probably don't like it. It's normal for children to start exhibiting likes and dislikes during this stage, so don't push the issue. Instead, find an alternative that has the same nutritional value as the rejected food. You can also disguise food by grating it into pasta sauces, mixing it with rice, mashing it into favourite vegetables or fruits, and including it in bakes. On nights when children simply refuse to eat, suggest they eat in their cubby house or on a blanket in the lounge room and make a picnic out of it – a change of atmosphere and a little food fun often helps.

Also at this stage of development, children can begin serving themselves. Children at this age will usually not overeat, stopping when they are full - unless they are made to clean their plate. Studies have shown that children encouraged to serve themselves tend to make decisions that are better for their bodies, such as healthier food choices and appropriate portion sizes – even when unsupervised and outside the home. Therefore, encouraging children to serve themselves allows them to determine how much food is the right amount for a serving, and whether they are hungry enough to need seconds.

Although preschool children's energy and nutrient needs are increasing as they grow, they still have fairly small appetites. Therefore, you should continue to feed your child 4-6 small meals or snacks throughout the day. Since your child doesn't eat much, these frequent meals should be rich in the nutrients they need. This type of meal schedule will result in an evenly elevated metabolism, rather than the highs and lows that 3 traditional meals tend to cause - which suits the preschooler's high energy levels perfectly.

Activity Requirements

During the preschool years, structured and unstructured play continues to be of great importance. Your child is old enough to begin learning that games have rules, and what it means to follow them. Children also have a great deal of energy at this stage.

The high energy levels and comprehension of this stage makes it a perfect opportunity for increased family activities. Through modelling and explaining the rules of a game, you can teach your children about healthy competition, fair play, and teamwork. As they learn these concepts, they will most likely start making up their own games; you should encourage their creativity by allowing them to do this, but use the opportunity to teach them more about rules by asking questions about their invented games. The most

important lesson you can teach your child is that active play and games are more about having fun and using your imagination than anything else.

Another method of encouraging healthy activity in your child during the preschool years is to assign chores. More than just teaching responsibility, simple tasks such as putting away toys or helping to set or clear the dinner table encourage other forms of activity. Children at this age are eager to please, and so should be supervised and encouraged, but never criticized.

Common Problems and Other Needs

Fostering complete wellbeing for your preschooler requires your attention in other matters, as well. Some other common issues your preschooler faces include:

- ✓ **Dental care** – The preschool years are a prime time to begin teaching the importance of oral care. Parents should teach their children the basics of brushing and flossing. Children at this age should be getting sufficient fluoride, either from tap water or supplements. Regular dentist visits are also important.

- ✓ **Faddy eating and food refusal** – Don't worry if your child starts refusing to eat certain foods; this phase is a normal part of childhood development. Continue to

offer regular meals and snacks with a variety of foods, keeping portion sizes small. Most importantly, try to remain calm and keep mealtime a fun experience for everyone. If the problem persists consult your family doctor or a nutritionist for further advice.

✓ **Tantrums** – Tantrums can be a frustrating behavioural issue for parents; however, they represent a normal phase of childhood development. The way you handle tantrums during this phase sets the stage for your child's emotional development and expectations later in life. Be consistent in setting and maintaining boundaries, but also realize that tantrums can erupt as a result of tiredness, hunger, or other conditions that are out of the child's control.

5 TO 12 YEARS

Between the ages of 5-12, children's bodies continue to go through many changes, at the end of which is adolescence. In addition, children's social environments undergo major changes during this period, and peer involvement becomes a much stronger factor. As a result, continued emphasis on communication, good nutrition and exercise is important.

Physical Growth and Development

Growth trends between ages 5-12 tend to be very individualized: some kids grow slowly throughout these years, catching their growth spurt in adolescence, while other kids get their growing done early. Because the body is rapidly developing into the form it will take in adulthood, it will develop around your child's current weight. In other words, any extra weight during this stage will raise the body's natural perception of its normal weight, making the weight hard for your child to lose in their teens and later in life.

"Exercise habits during this stage will determine the composition of your child's body later in life. An active child will have an increased metabolic rate, fewer fat cells, and increased bone density, a benefit that will carry on into adulthood."

In the same vein, exercise habits during this stage will determine the composition of your child's body later in life. An active child will have an increased metabolic rate, fewer fat cells, and increased bone density - benefits that will carry on into adulthood.

Puberty, which begins late in this stage of development, introduces many new changes in your child's body. Because puberty means rapid growth and development, proper nutrition and exercise is especially important.

Social and Emotional Development

Because children in this stage are now in school, their societal influences have broadened to include peers and other adult caregivers, such as teachers and coaches. Peer relationships are especially important, as emotional development and self-esteem depends heavily on peer acceptance. Children also begin to develop a sense of social conscience during the primary school years.

This stage of development is also marked by many mood swings and the testing of boundaries. It is especially important to establish firm boundaries, upholding them with consequences when they are crossed. However, it's also important to show your children you are there for them when they need you.

Nutritional Requirements

Because school age children eat at least one meal each day with friends instead of family, they will almost certainly show the effects of this new influence. Peer pressure and the influence of the media help steer them toward unhealthy food choices while at school. In order to maintain a healthy diet, it is vital that good nutrition continue to be emphasized at home.

It is important to realize that as the parent, you no longer have control over the meals eaten at school. Children can choose what they want to eat from school cafeterias, trade or discard the contents of bag lunches, or purchase junk food from vending machines at school. Since children at this stage are generally not yet conscious of body image, they make their food choices according to taste and values instilled by advertising gimmicks or peer pressure. Instead of fighting a losing battle to maintain control over these meals, combat these new influences by continuing to instil in your child the value of healthy food choices and involving them in packed lunch preparation and choice.

Good nutrition is particularly important as children approach adolescence, as adequate nutritional support is required for the proper development and release of hormones, and muscle and bone growth. Children in this stage need a wide range of nutrients, especially iron, calcium, vitamin C, and folate; their diets should include a healthy balance of proteins and carbohydrates, as well as a limited amount of fats. Small, frequent meals and snacks are still beneficial.

Activity Requirements

In middle childhood, most children exercise through active play. Sports and physical education provide structured play, while recess and play dates allow for unstructured play. However, because your child may be increasingly driven to sedentary play such as video games, you may need to limit the time your child spends in front of the television or computer.

Family activities are especially important during this period. As children enter adolescence, they tend to become more resistant to family activities, and less interested in pleasing their parents. Therefore, the primary school years may be your last opportunity to help your child form healthy habits through family exercise.

Chores remain a solid way to promote responsibility and activity in your child. At this point, more complex – and more meaningful – chores are possible. For instance, putting your child in charge of planting and maintaining a garden both promotes exercise and helps teach good nutrition. Washing the car and cleaning up around the house are also valuable activities.

Common Problems and Other Needs

Other areas of your child's development that may require your attention include dental and emotional health, for example:

✓ **Continued dental hygiene** – Continue to stress the importance of oral health during this stage of development. With your child's permanent teeth coming in, brushing and flossing are more important than ever.

✓ **School influence and peer pressure** – Although most children love school, they sometimes suffer separation anxiety. Even as they adjust to the long days away from home and parents, your children may encounter peer pressure, the anxiety of making (or losing) friends, and other emotional challenges. To help children

adapt to new places, roles and people, it is important to make your home a secure, stable environment, and to demonstrate your interest in their lives with lots of encouragement and open lines of communication.

✔ **Bed-wetting** – Bed-wetting is an experience shared by many school age children in Australia, with boys being more prone to it than girls. Children who wet the bed only occasionally may do so as a result of stress; in these cases, parents should take care to find out what is bothering their child, and talk to them about it. However, children who wet the bed chronically might do so because they sleep too deeply or because their urinary system is not yet fully developed, making them literally unable to control their bladder functions during the night. Your doctor can offer a variety of medications and behavioural treatments for chronic bed-wetting; however, it is also important to maintain a loving, supportive, and communicative environment, as bed-wetting can have a serious impact on your child's self-esteem.

QUICK TIPS FOR PARENTS

✔ Maintain firm boundaries for your child, but don't hesitate to show emotional support as well.
✔ Continue to emphasize good nutrition at home.
✔ Pack and encourage healthy school food choices.
✔ Discourage too much time playing video games or watching TV.
✔ Organize family activities.
✔ Assign more complex chores.
✔ Emphasize brushing and flossing to care for permanent teeth.
✔ Be mindful of new school experiences and peer pressures.

12 TO 18 YEARS

During the teenage years, parental influence can be almost completely replaced by peer pressure and media influence. At the same time, teenagers' rapidly changing bodies require a great deal of energy, nutrients, and exercise. To counter the factors that distract teens from making healthy living choices, family encouragement and involvement become more important than ever.

Physical Growth and Development

During the teen years, you'll notice your child begins to look less like a child and more like an adult. Although individual development dictates different times for these changes to take place in each child, kids typically reach their adult height by their mid-teens. Hormonal levels reach their peak during this time as well, triggering rapid sexual and muscular development. Any excessive weight gain or weight loss may indicate an eating disorder, so parents need to remain especially attentive.

Emotional and Social Development

During the teen years, you may notice your child starting to adopt adult characteristics on an emotional level as well as physically. However, it is important to remember that teenagers are still not yet adults, and cannot be expected to make infallible decisions. The struggle for independence and peer influences may lead to outright rebellion, making firm boundaries and consequences for broken rules still necessary. However, involving teens in family decisions can help make them feel important and teach them good decision-making skills.

Often, your teen's peer network almost completely replaces the influence you once wielded as a parent. However, welcoming friends, holding BBQ's and parties, and getting to know your teenager's peers can help alleviate some of the isolation parents may feel during this stage. Body image may also become a virtual obsession, especially for girls. As your teenager struggles to lose weight or gain muscle, his or her self-worth assessment becomes dependent on peer opinions and media-established norms.

As social pressures become more dominant, experimentation with sex, alcohol, and drugs may also become a problem. Although as a parent you cannot be present at all times to monitor your teen's behaviour, the values you have modelled and instilled since early childhood can have a strong impact on the choices your teenager makes. Open communication and encouragement continue to be important.

Nutritional Requirements

Rapid growth and development during the teenage years require not simply a lot of food, but good nutrition as well. Teens may find that they can eat more than adults, leading them to believe they can eat anything they want. However, it's important to continue to stress the value of a balanced nutritional plan, as nutrients and the quality consumed are extremely important for your teen's continual development.

Because of the emphasis on body image during this period, many teens may become concerned with their weight. Weight loss techniques are often unhealthy: skipping meals, fasting, and following fad diets are common ways of attempting to lose weight. When teenagers want to diet, they should first be encouraged to analyze their weight objectively and determine if they really need to lose weight. If they do, encourage them to control their weight with healthy food choices and exercise.

Activity Requirements

Although the rapidity of development means that activity is more important than ever, the teenage years pose a threat to continued exercise habits. Teen socialization has become a much more sedentary activity in recent years, thanks to mobile phones and the Internet. Also, more teenagers have cars than in the old days, enabling them to get from place to place without the exercise it used to require. In addition, physical education requirements have been cut dramatically, making school almost completely sedentary for most teens these days.

"Rapid growth and development during the teenage years require not simply a lot of food, but good nutrition as well. Teens may find that they can eat more than adults, leading them to believe they can eat anything they want. However, it's important to continue to stress the value of a balanced nutritional plan."

Organized sport is also far more competitive than it used to be, alienating a lot of kids who would have played for the fun of the game - rather than a future as a professional athlete. Teens who hold jobs are also particularly disadvantaged, as their jobs are usually sedentary and reduce free time that could be spent in active play; additionally, many teen jobs are in the fast food industry, which results in an increase in fatty foods in their diets.

However, teens tend to continue physical activity according to habits they formed earlier in childhood. In other words, the efforts you've made over the years to teach your child the value of regular exercise will now come to fruition. Even so, sedentary pastimes should be discouraged as much as possible, and teens should be encouraged to engage in active play.

Common Problems and Other Needs

Your teen is coming into contact with a great many new pressures, which have an impact on continued physical and emotional development. To guide your teen safely through this tumultuous time, it's important to understand some of the other influences that he or she faces:

- ✓ **Understanding sexuality** – Puberty brings with it physical and emotional changes that may overwhelm your teenager. Because of the seriousness of these changes in your teen's physical and emotional makeup - and often the added peer pressures - you should strive to maintain good communication and a supportive home life. Girls begin menstruating at this stage, which not only requires emotional adjustment, but also increased nutritional focus to ensure sufficient amounts of iron and other essential nutrients.

- ✓ **Slimming** – There is an enormous pressure on today's teens to have a specific body type, and in order to achieve the ideal, many adopt unnecessary and unhealthy diets. Numerous studies have reported that teenagers, especially girls, are dissatisfied with their weight, and have low self-esteem and a distorted view of their body image. It's important to communicate with your teen about healthy body image and habits; and to watch for signs of eating disorders such as anorexia, bulimia, and bingeing. If your teen wants to slim, proper nutrition and regular exercise are the best methods.

- ✓ **Acne** – Contrary to popular belief, there's little scientific evidence that acne is caused or exacerbated by fatty and sugary foods. Hormonal factors, including stress, are the most likely cause. However, proper nutrition can improve the overall health of skin: zinc, vitamins A, C, and E, and plenty of water are important ingredients for healthy skin. There are also medical treatments for acne, ranging from facial cleansers for mild blemishes to dermatological medications for more severe acne. Consult your family doctor or a dermatologist for help.

QUICK TIPS FOR PARENTS

- ✓ Maintain behavioural boundaries.
- ✓ Stress the value of good nutrition.
- ✓ Involve teens in shopping and meal preparation.
- ✓ Encourage healthy food choices and exercise as alternatives to dieting.
- ✓ Emphasize the value of exercise.
- ✓ Make an effort to meet your teen's friends.
- ✓ Treat your teen with love and encouragement, keeping communication lines open.

CONTINUING DEVELOPMENT

Although society officially recognizes individuals as adults at age 18, physical development does not stop then. However, the parents' influence is considerably diminished at that point, which makes it even more imperative that parents instil healthy values in their children, beginning at an early age.

3

Food for Thought

Understanding and solving weight problems

Quick Chapter Guide

- ✔ Understanding the facts about weight problems
- ✔ Self-assessment at home – tools for deciding if there is a weight problem
- ✔ The mirror test, the pinch test, BMI and energy assessment
- ✔ Dieting is not the answer – diets don't work!
- ✔ Promoting lifestyle changes to improve family nutrition and activity levels
- ✔ The importance of starting small
- ✔ Keys to successful change
- ✔ Finding motivation
- ✔ The value of healthy habits

Food For Thought

Understanding and solving weight problems

In Australia and the UK, one in five children and adolescents are either overweight or obese, and at the current rate, researchers predict these figures will rise to more than 50% by 2020. In the majority of cases the growing incidence of weight problems stems from the trend toward a higher consumption of more convenient (and less healthy) foods, and less active lifestyles.

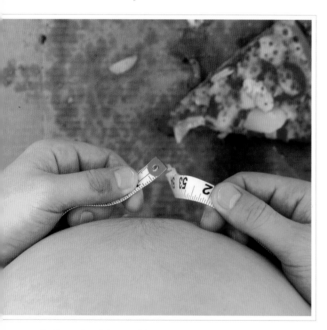

So how should we address this rapidly growing tendency toward overweight? Despite modern society's fascination with fad dieting, weight issues are most successfully dealt with by making lifelong changes to diet and exercise habits. And although our primary concern should be reversing the trend in our children, by definition this requires a good, hard look at our own habits. Obese or overweight parents frequently raise obese or overweight children, making weight a family problem – and a family problem requires a family solution.

HOW DO I DETERMINE IF THERE IS A WEIGHT PROBLEM?

The first step in addressing a weight problem is determining if there truly is one. Stepping on the scale isn't as accurate an assessment as you might think, since the scale doesn't differentiate between bone, muscle and fat. In order to truly identify a weight problem, you need to know how much fat your body carries.

There are a number of tests to determine body fat and identify weight problems, some of which can be done at home. Despite the temptation to frequently check your progress, you should only test every month or two, since body fat assessments will not show subtle changes. Testing too frequently will mean that you won't see any immediate results, which can be discouraging, to say the least.

The Mirror Test

One of the best tests for fatness is the simplest and is what nutritionists call the eyeball test. Stand in front of a mirror in your underwear and look objectively at your body for the amount of muscle versus fat. If you see only muscle definition, it's safe to assume you don't have a weight problem. However, if you look in the mirror and see soft rolls that shouldn't be there, such as around your stomach, under your chin, or on your legs, it's safe to say you may be an unhealthy weight.

Looking objectively at our figure can have a far greater impact than simply staring down at a bunch of numbers on a scale, and allows us to look at our body and take note of how healthy our appearance may or may not be. After a little progress has been made, it's very satisfying to revisit the mirror and appreciate a reduction in our body fat, better looking body curves and improved muscle tone. For these reasons, the mirror test can be a great motivator, especially for adolescents, teens and adults - who tend to be more body image conscious than younger children.

Visual Guidelines for the Pinch Test

A — Low body fat
Optimal weight range

B — Some body fat
Still within range

C — Excess body fat
Considered overweight

D — Far too much body fat
Considered obese

Can You Pinch More Than an Inch?

Another simple self-assessment technique is a test called the pinch test, which tests the thickness of a fold of skin.

To perform the pinch test on yourself or your child:

- ✓ Pinch a little piece of flesh in the tummy, about 2.5cm on either side of the belly button, and pull the skin away slightly. Don't squeeze until it hurts. Just make sure that you have a firm hold on the flesh you want to measure using your thumb and forefinger.
- ✓ Using a ruler, measure the distance between the skin of your thumb and the skin of your forefinger.
- ✓ Repeat the test on the side of your child's stomach directly above the hip in line with the belly button.
- ✓ Fat deposits vary from site to site around your body. For greater accuracy, you can do this test all over your body including the fleshy areas around the back of the thighs and under the raised arms.

If you can pinch more than an inch then you or your child are probably overweight.

Height and Weight Assessment - BMI - What's Your Number?

Although stepping on the scale isn't as accurate an assessment as once thought, when used in combination with height measurements and other tests, it can be a useful tool to assist parents in tracking and reviewing weight loss. The combination of height and weight assessment is commonly known as the body mass index (BMI).

Although BMI provides a useful method of weight-to-height comparison, the test does not differentiate between body fat and muscle mass. For instance, a heavily muscled individual will weigh more, and therefore will have a BMI in the overweight or obese range – despite the lack of fat on their body. The test is also less than accurate for elderly people who tend to have low muscle mass, and people who are shorter than normal in stature.

A child or adolescent's BMI is determined by dividing their weight (kilograms) by their height squared (m^2). The table below gives cut-off points for children considered to be in the overweight and obese range. Remember these are only averages.

BMI GUIDELINES FOR CHILDREN CONSIDERED OVERWEIGHT OR OBESE

BMI and overweight:
Children above these cut-off points are considered overweight

Age	Girls	Boys
2 year olds	18.02	18.41
5 year olds	17.15	17.42
10 year olds	19.86	19.84
15 year olds	23.94	23.29
18 year olds and over	25	25

BMI and obesity:
Children above these cut-off points are considered obese

Age	Girls	Boys
2 year olds	19.81	20.09
5 year olds	19.17	19.3
10 year olds	24.11	24
15 year olds	29.11	28.30
18 year olds and over	30	30

*Source: 2006 Better Health Channel: Victorian Government Dept. Human Services

If you have trouble calculating BMI go to
www.abcfitkids.com/bmicalculator
and use the online calculator for kids.

Energy requirements vary with age and just as a child's weight may vary during different developmental stages, so do their energy needs. For instance, an infant only needs approximately 2,700 kilojoules a day, whereas a toddler needs 4,400 or greater. By the time your child reaches adolescence, they'll require slightly more kilojoules than the average adult. Factors other than your child's stage of development also determine energy needs, for example, girls normally need fewer kilojoules each day than boys do. The metabolism, body type and amount of physical activity your child engages in will also make a difference to the amount of energy their body requires.

The table below will help you compare the average daily energy needs of your child with their daily energy intake (based on the amount and type of food they eat).

Average Daily Energy Requirements for Children (kJ/Day)		
Age	Boys	Girls
1 month	2,000	1,800
6 months	2,700	2,500
12 months	3,500	3,200
2 years	4,400	4,200
3 years	6,300	5,800
5 years	7,000	6,500
7 years	7,800	7,300
9 years	8,800	8,200
11 years	9,900	9,000
13 years	11,200	10,000
15 years	12,600	10,600
18 years	14,000	10,900

* Source: 2005 National Health & Medical Research Council of Australia

** Daily energy values in the table above are based on moderately active children within each age range who participate in about 1 hour of exercise a day (excluding infants and toddlers).

Beware of Averages - Individual Variations All Play a Role

When judging body fat and weight problems in children, it's important to remember that different factors come into play during physical growth and development. These factors may include developmental stage, growth spurts, gender, and ethnic variations. For this reason, the more tests you use to assess potential weight problems the better.

If you are at all unsure about your assessment of your child's weight, contact your doctor or a nutritionist for help.

You-Are-What-You-Eat Factor - Daily Energy Needs vs Intake

Parents often ask how many kilojoules (energy) their children need, but for the average child who is growing and developing normally and enjoys regular activity and healthy food choices, counting kilojoules is usually not necessary. However, knowing how much energy your child needs each day can help you plan your child's nutrition and make sure they are eating a healthy diet. Being familiar with energy requirements can also be helpful in evaluating children who are gaining weight and for children who are overweight.

Use a food diary and the information from food labels to check your children's average daily energy intake compared to their likely needs. Chart eating habits over several days for a more accurate snapshot of your average kilojoule intake.

An energy assessment can be an important first step in understanding why you or your children may be overweight. It may be that you are just not active enough to burn away your daily food intake, or you may be eating too many fats or too much food and consequently adding too many kilojoules even if you are active.

It's useful to know that 1 kilogram of body fat contains the equivalent of 37,000kJ, so to lose 1kg of body fat in a week, you would need to burn an additional 37,000kJ, or about 5000kJ a day. Of course it's healthier to lose weight over a longer period of time so a more realistic approach would be to aim to lose the kilo of fat gradually over 4-6 weeks.

QUICK TIPS FOR PARENTS

✓ The scale alone doesn't present an accurate assessment of weight problems.

✓ Body mass index (BMI) provides a fair indication of whether you are at an appropriate weight for your height, but doesn't take into consideration factors such as muscle mass.

✓ A visual test looks for rolls of excess fat, which signify a weight problem.

✓ The pinch test measures the thickness of a pinch of skin; if you can pinch more than an inch, your weight needs attention.

✓ An energy assessment can be an important first step in understanding why you or your children may be over weight.

✓ Relying on a combination of tests is more accurate when assessing weight problems and reviewing progress.

✓ Be positive and encouraging when assessing weight and body image.

✓ Once on a program, test your child's weight every 6-8 weeks and aim for small, incremental changes.

✓ When retesting weight, morning time is best, and try to keep the intervals regular.

✓ Consult your doctor or a nutritionist if you are unsure, or if your child suffers from rapid weight loss or gain.

WHAT KINDS OF CHANGES DO I NEED TO MAKE?

The prospect of changing to a healthier lifestyle may seem daunting. Many people are reluctant to embark on what they see as a very long, difficult, and rarely successful journey. Realistically, however, you only need to make changes to two areas of your family's life: diet and exercise.

Changing Your Diet

When it comes to healthy living, diet is very important. Most weight gain in children and adults is a result of consuming far more kilojoules (energy) than required.

Energy intake should be determined by the individual's level of activity.

The quality of one's diet is also significant. With the influx of convenience and fast foods in our society, many people don't get the nutrients their bodies need – even though they are eating more than ever. To combat this problem, make sure you feed your family a combination of fresh fruits and vegetables, grains, lean meat, and dairy products. Cooking meals from scratch and reading product labels are two habits to get into, as they allow you to know – and control – what is going into your family's food. Involving the family in meal planning and preparation can help galvanize them into action by making them feel personally committed to the ultimate goal of a healthier lifestyle.

Special dietary considerations are also important, as children's needs vary as they grow. For instance, in very young children, only 30-35% of total energy should come from fat; in children and teens age four and up, only 25-35% of total energy should come from fat. These figures are very different from those for adults, who should get 25% or less of their daily energy from fat.

Adding Activity

Activity is just as important a part of healthy living as diet, yet it is often overlooked by fad dieters. Your activity output – the amount of energy you burn each day – should match your energy intake, as any excess energy will be stored as fat. Regular activity helps maintain a healthy weight; builds strong bones and muscles; promotes good posture and balance; improves fitness; and has a positive influence on mood and self-esteem – for kids and adults alike. It's also a very social activity.

For optimum growth and development, children should have at least 1 hour of physical activity every day. Start by adding 30 minutes of moderate activity three or four times a week and then build from there. Activity can be as simple as a brisk walk together; shooting hoops in the back yard; doing floor exercises or dancing to music; bike riding around the neighbourhood park; playing on the jungle gym together; or swimming in the local pool. Talk to your children about enrolling them in a school or community sports program that interests them, for example dance and martial arts classes, yoga or team sports.

QUICK TIPS FOR PARENTS

- ✓ Diet and exercise are the two primary areas that need attention when making the shift to a healthier lifestyle.
- ✓ A good diet is made up of quantity and quality: the appropriate energy intake, combined with fresh, nutrient-rich food choices.
- ✓ To maintain an ideal health and weight, children need at least 1 hour of physical activity every day.
- ✓ Start with small changes to diet and exercise.
- ✓ Begin with smaller portion sizes and by excluding one or two poor food choices a week and replacing them with healthier alternatives.
- ✓ Add 30 minutes of moderate activity three times a week and build from there.

HOW DO I KNOW MY CHANGES WILL SUCCEED?

Once you have an idea of how to proceed with making the shift to a healthier lifestyle, your hardest task will be to convince your child. Many children are reluctant to eat right and exercise more, since these changes require giving up a routine that they may feel perfectly happy with. However, with the right amount of patience, persistence, and family involvement, your child is bound to come around.

As with anything worth doing, improving your family's health will take some work. Don't let that scare you, though. The key is to introduce changes slowly, rather than staging a crash course in dieting. Knowing how to motivate your family will make your efforts easier, as well.

Remember the Answer Is Not Dieting - Diets Don't Work

Just about everyone has tried dieting at least once – and has experienced the disappointment of failing to keep the diet. The truth is, diets just don't work. They fail to make lifelong changes, and as a result the dieter gains the weight back immediately after going off the diet. And because of the extremes diets go to, maintaining one over the long term is virtually impossible.

Diets operate on an ideal that often hovers just above starvation. Dieters are encouraged to substitute a shake for a meal or restrict themselves to just one or two types of food. Although the sudden drop in kilojoule intake encourages the dieter's body to burn excess fat as energy instead of food, the near-starvation plan is difficult to maintain, and sooner or later the diet will be broken. This causes a yo-yo effect in the frequent dieter's weight, which is extremely detrimental to their health and self-esteem.

The biggest reason that diets fail is that they try to reverse in a matter of weeks or months a trend that has often been progressing for years. They also tend to ignore the need for exercise or healthy food choices, making immediate weight loss their only goal. As a result, diets teach next to nothing about developing lifelong healthy habits. The goal of changing one's lifestyle should be to introduce small changes slowly, practicing them every hour of every day until they become second nature. Only then can permanent weight loss, and the related health benefits, become a reality.

Of special concern is the teen dieter. During a period when the body is rapidly growing and changing, many teens restrict their energy intake beyond reason. This deprives their bodies of nutrients essential to healthy development. If you are worried your teen is crash dieting, or has some form of eating disorder, talk openly with them about it and encourage healthier alternatives.

Start Small

For you and your family to stick with the changes you are instituting, it's important not to overwhelm everyone with sudden, drastic changes. Start with small goals: eating less fat per meal, cutting back on portion sizes, adding thirty minutes of exercise two or more days per week, or even watching less television each day. Although you may not see immediate weight loss, rest assured that even these small changes carry significant health benefits.

As everyone becomes comfortable with these changes, you can add new, more challenging goals, gradually easing you and your family into a new, healthier lifestyle. Reading nutrition information labels and cooking meals yourself allows you to control what goes into your family's food; eating smaller, more frequent meals maintains an even metabolic rate; family activity becomes a tradition instead of a chore. As you move on to more significant goals such as these, you will begin to notice changes in you and your family's weight and overall health, as well as the feelings of freedom and confidence that come with achieving your goals.

Here are the keys to successful change:

✓ **Develop Awareness:** Involve the whole family in the process of self-assessment. Children will be more motivated if they play a part in the decision making and are aware of how "inactive" they may be. Just like a food diary, keeping an activity journal for a week is a great way for children and adults to assess their normal weekly activity levels.

✓ **Set Goals:** Set small achievable goals for the whole family focused around eating habits, rest and activity levels. Assess goals regularly and revise the goal when needed. Review new eating and exercise commitments at least every week, and weight loss progress every 6-8 weeks.

✓ **Get Agreement on the Plan:** Talk over the nutritional and activity goals with the whole family to encourage everyone to stick to the plan and work together towards achieving healthy change.

✓ **Praise and encouragement are important:** Give feedback and praise on a daily basis; talk about goals to reinforce what needs to be done and how to get there.

✓ **Recognize and Reward Change:** Reinforce new behaviour and celebrate successes through recognition and rewards.

Finding Motivation

You may be thinking, "I'll never be able to get my family to commit to a healthier lifestyle." However, it's easier than you think to motivate people to eat better and exercise more frequently.

One of the strongest motivators is, of course, fun. If you and your family are having a good time, it won't even be a struggle to implement changes in your lifestyle. Grocery shopping, planning meals, and cooking together can make eating right enjoyable for everyone. On the same note, playing with your kids is much more fun than going to the gym – and it's more fun for your kids than playing alone, too. Family activities such as these teach children – and their parents – that a healthy lifestyle doesn't have to be a boring lifestyle.

Self-esteem can be a natural motivator, as well. Although an overweight child may suffer from low self-esteem, succeeding in meeting their goals and losing weight will do wonders for improving self-image. Before long, activities that took a lot of coaxing at first will begin to be met with acceptance, even enthusiasm! As your child's self-esteem improves, so will their willingness to make the switch to a healthier lifestyle.

Praise and rewards also make great motivators. Praise and rewards can be used to recognize individual achievements, but rewards can also be given to the entire family when certain goals are met. However, be careful not to use food or television privileges as rewards, as this will prove counterproductive to your ultimate goal of a healthier lifestyle.

Although progress can make a great motivator, discourage family members from checking weight or body fat too frequently. Changes may take a while to register physically, creating discouragement instead of feelings of accomplishment and motivation. Instead, encourage family members to gauge progress through the achievement of smaller, more readily attainable goals.

QUICK TIPS FOR PARENTS

✓ Dieting focuses on short-term benefits, whereas switching to a healthier lifestyle is long-term.
✓ In the beginning, set small goals so as not to overwhelm yourself or your family. As you achieve them, you can set new, more complex goals.
✓ Focus on smaller portion sizes, less fat and sugar.
✓ Increase activity three times a week for 30 minutes or more.
✓ Make use of natural motivators, such as having fun, giving praise and rewards, and highlighting progress.
✓ Chart your progress and make change a family affair.
✓ If you need help consult your family doctor or a nutritionist.

THE VALUE OF HEALTHY HABITS

Recognizing that you or your child has a weight problem is a difficult but necessary step to making the switch to a healthier lifestyle. However, once you've identified the problem and taken steps toward creating a healthier environment for you and your family, you'll quickly find that the benefits far outweigh the steps it took to get you there.

If you need additional help to get started, or resources like printable food and activity diaries, go to
www.abcfitkids.com/foodactivitydiaries

4

Food Monsters

Other common food related problems

Quick Chapter Guide

- ✔ Understanding food allergies, typical problem foods and common symptoms
- ✔ Identifying and managing food Intolerance
- ✔ Food monsters - colourings, preservatives and flavour enhancers to avoid
- ✔ Identifying and preventing dehydration in children
- ✔ Understanding the links between food additives and attention disorders
- ✔ How to use a food elimination program
- ✔ The added benefits of exercise

Food Monsters

Other common food related problems

What would you say if someone told you that you may be able to treat your child's behavioural issues with diet and exercise? It might sound far-fetched, but if you think about it, nutrition and physical activity is often used to treat medical conditions such as diabetes, cholesterol, and heart disease. So why should it be such a surprise if the benefits extend to other conditions, as well?

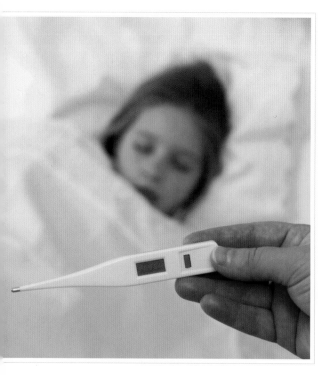

Generations ago, people lived entirely on fresh produce, meat, and home-made grains, and the incidence of problems such as attention disorders, anxiety, and asthma was almost unheard of - yet today, health problems like

these affect many of our children and the incidence is rising. What has changed? For starters, children are far less active than they used to be which generally means they are less physically healthy and tend to have weaker immune systems and less resilience to stress. Secondly, children's increased consumption of convenience foods and the food industry's growing reliance on food colourings, preservatives and additives corresponds with the rise in frequency of conditions such as attention disorders, diabetes, depression, anxiety, asthma, and lethargy.

In many cases a simple change in diet and exercise have been shown to afford great benefits to many children suffering from these and other ailments. This chapter aims to inform parents about the more common presenting symptoms children may have when reacting adversely to food ingredients and additives - while highlighting some of the food monsters to avoid.

FOOD ALLERGIES

Although we don't know why food allergies happen, we do know that an allergic reaction involves the body's immune system. For some reason, some people's immune systems attack certain foods. Although the resulting physical reaction can seem scary, it may help to have a solid understanding of the symptoms and possible causes.

Identifying Food Allergies

Allergic reactions typically happen very fast - within 30 minutes to 2 hours - which can be rather alarming. Symptoms of an allergic reaction include itching or a rash, swelling around the face and neck, vomiting, and diarrhoea. The most severe allergic reaction, anaphylaxis, can occur within moments, and causes blood pressure to drop and breathing to become laboured. Anaphylaxis also frequently causes the child to lose consciousness.

Because the symptoms come on very suddenly and are often quite severe, food allergies are fairly easy to identify. If you are unsure speak with your child's doctor about your concerns. If your child has a severe reaction to food seek medical attention immediately.

Typical Problem Foods

There are certain allergies that are very common in children, such as allergies to peanuts, wheat gluten, and cow's milk. Although children usually grow out of the allergies they exhibit in childhood, some allergies – such as peanut allergies – will likely remain throughout the individual's life. Also, allergies to some foods are extremely severe, requiring that the child carry emergency medication that will delay the reaction if he or she accidentally ingests the food.

Eliminating Problem Foods

It is generally pretty easy to cut certain foods from your child's diet at home, especially when the seriousness of the allergy leaves no other choice. However, meals eaten away from home may pose a problem. Most schools and childcare centres are conscientious about food allergies, but you may still want to discuss the issue with them in detail. Some allergies, such as peanut allergies, can be so serious that the child cannot even breathe peanut particles without having a reaction. Depending on the strength of your child's allergy, simply sending your child to school or day-care with a packed lunch may suffice; or you may

need to request that the food item be eliminated from the kitchen entirely.

In order to eliminate certain foods from your child's diet, you may need to become an avid reader of nutrition information labels. Certain foods show up in the most unlikely places. For example, peanut oil is contained in many snacks and treats, even when the flavour is not described as peanut. Wheat gluten is also contained in many food products. Reading food labels may seem a hassle, but it is a habit that can save your child from much discomfort.

QUICK TIPS FOR PARENTS

- ✔ Monitor children's behaviour closely after they have tried new foods.
- ✔ When medical problems arise, keep an open mind to the possibility of food allergies.
- ✔ Avoid food additives, especially those that have been known to cause allergic reactions.
- ✔ Eliminate foods and additives that you suspect to have caused an allergic reaction in your child.
- ✔ Learn to read food labels to exclude any problem ingredients.

FOOD INTOLERANCE

Food intolerance is frequently confused with food allergy; however, it is a very different physical reaction. A food intolerance reaction is a chemical response within the body, rather than the immune response of a food allergy. Food intolerances are also typically not as severe; however, they are much more common than food allergies, and much less frequently identified.

Identifying Food Intolerance

The presentation of food intolerance symptoms are usually delayed, sometimes by as much as 48 hours, making it more difficult to make the connection. The reaction is also not as serious as a food allergy, although the severity often is related to the amount of food eaten. Symptoms of food intolerance can be similar to food allergies – itching, swelling, diarrhoea, vomiting – but they can also include behavioural issues, such as hyperactivity and lethargy. Because of the delayed response and obscure connection to the food eaten, many food intolerance symptoms are misdiagnosed as conditions such as asthma, attention disorders, and depression.

Typical Problem Foods

Food intolerance is much more common than most people realize. However, there are a few food intolerances that are more common than others.

- ✓ **Cow's milk** – Although we know that an allergy to cow's milk is a result of the protein contained in it, it is unclear what causes the intolerance to cow's milk. Look for irritability, diarrhoea, and vomiting.
- ✓ **Lactose** – Lactose intolerance occurs when the individual's body is unable to completely digest lactose, a sugar found in milk, due to a lack of the necessary enzymes in the digestive tract. Look for upset stomach, increased gas, white diarrhoea, headache, and fatigue.
- ✓ **Shellfish** – This intolerance is usually limited to shellfish, and is caused by bacteria inside the shells. Look for general discomfort and red, hot skin.

In addition to difficulties with certain types of food, studies have shown that many children have intolerances to the colourings and additives used in food.

Below is a list of the most common culprits known to cause children's medical and behavioural problems, such as asthma, skin rashes, and attention disorders:

Food colourings:
- ✗ Tartrazine (102)
- ✗ Sunset Yellow (110)
- ✗ Amaranth (123)
- ✗ Erythrosine (127)
- ✗ Annatto extracts (160b)
- ✗ Carmoisine (122)
- ✗ Ponceau 4R (124)

Preservatives:
- ✗ Sodium benzoate (211)
- ✗ Sulphur dioxide (220)
- ✗ Calcium propionate (282)
- ✗ Antioxidants: BHA or butylated hydroxyanisole (320)

Flavour enhancers:
- ✗ MSG or monosodium glutamate (621)
- ✗ Disodium 5'-ribonucleotides (635)
- ✗ Artificial sweetener aspartame (951)

Although many people still routinely deny the effect these additives can have, studies have been done that show the connection.

A recent European study tested the effects of food additives on 277 three-year-olds over the course of a month and found that artificial colourings (102, 110, 122, 124), and benzoate preservative (211) caused significant behavioural effects observed by parents including 'interrupting', 'fiddling with objects', 'disturbing others', 'difficulty settling down to sleep' and 'temper tantrums' - whether there was an existing history of hyperactivity or not.

It's also important to realize that reactions to these chemicals may not be limited to a few individuals, as some studies on MSG have shown; MSG can cause a reaction in anyone if they eat enough of it.

Eliminating Problem Foods

Intolerances to food additives can be particularly dangerous because most people don't make the connection. Problems resulting from these additives can go on for years if the connection is not made. Therefore, it is best to eliminate the possibility of a food intolerance before moving on to more invasive treatments.

It is important to note that although the symptoms can cause your child discomfort – and cause you concern – food intolerance conditions are completely avoidable. It is not all that difficult to eliminate a problem food from your child's diet, and what little trouble it does cause is made up for by the benefits to your child. In particular, the troublesome additives listed above should be avoided at all costs - the number codes for additives and colourings are listed on food labels so read labels carefully.

QUICK TIPS FOR PARENTS

✓ Monitor children's behaviour closely after they have tried new foods.

✓ Always consider the potential connection between behavioural issues and food intolerance.

✓ Eliminate foods and additives that you suspect your child is intolerant to.

✓ There is no need to remember the names of nasty additives or colours - simply make a list of the numbers and check food labels before buying packaged products.

For a wallet-size Food Monster Fact Sheet, visit
www.abcfitkids.com/foodmonsterfacts

DEHYDRATION

Believe it or not, dehydration can have a significant impact on your child's physical and behavioural health. Although most discussions of proper nutrition overlook the importance of water, hydration plays a very important part in the body's functions. Water keeps the airways moist enough to function properly; if your child does not drink enough water, the airways will dry up, allowing allergens and irritants into the lungs. Also, water is necessary to help the body metabolize food properly; and because the brain is 80% water, sufficient hydration is needed for proper brain function.

Identifying Dehydration

If your child is dehydrated, he or she may exhibit a lack of energy that could otherwise be taken for depression or lethargy. Also, dehydration can lead to asthmatic symptoms, such as coughing and wheezing.

Preventing Dehydration

Despite the severity of its symptoms, dehydration is easy to prevent. You should encourage your child to drink plenty of water throughout the day. However, note that children and adults with asthma should avoid drinking cold water, as it can cause spasms in the bronchial tubes, thereby triggering an asthma attack.

Although it may be tempting to count your child's juice or soft drink – or your coffee or tea – toward your goal of staying hydrated, keep in mind that these fluids are not water, and should not be substituted for it. Juice and soft drink contribute significantly to daily energy intake, and soft drink – both diet and regular – contains many unhealthy food colourings and additives. Additionally, coffee and tea are diuretics, which siphon water out of your body and into your urine, actually dehydrating you further.

QUICK TIPS FOR PARENTS

- ✔ Look for signs of dehydration, such as coughing or lethargy.
- ✔ Encourage your child to drink water frequently, especially when they are engaged in active play.
- ✔ Room temperature water is easiest on the body.
- ✔ Avoid substituting other drinks for water.

ATTENTION DISORDERS

One of the most disturbing problems facing our children today is the apparent epidemic of attention disorders. Studies estimate that 3-6% of school-aged children in the UK, Australia and the US suffer from attention disorders. While this is alarming, the current trend of treating attention disorders with central nervous system stimulants such as methylphenidate (Ritalin) is more disturbing; particularly when more natural approaches to treatment do exist – and considering the growing evidence that a proportion of cases may be due to food intolerance rather than any direct neurological dysfunction.

Alternative treatments based on diet assessment, nutritional supplementation and exercise have been shown to be very effective for many children suffering from attention disorders and should be considered before drug therapy.

Identifying Attention Disorders

ADHD is characterized by two separate types of symptoms: inattention and hyperactivity. If you believe your child is demonstrating symptoms of ADHD, it may be helpful to talk to your family doctor; however, be cautious and remain open to exploring the role of diet in your child's symptoms.

Treating Attention Disorders through Diet

Attempting to treat attention disorders like ADHD through diet can be difficult, especially in light of the availability of food at school and in other places where you cannot monitor your child's choices. However, the obvious benefits to your child make the trouble worthwhile. Among the many proposed causes of attention disorders are dietary concerns, such as food colourings and other additives, food intolerance, and nutrient depletions. Therefore, eliminating harmful substances from your child's diet should come before any attempt to control behaviour through medication.

The basis to treating attention disorders naturally is a sound nutritional plan. By replacing convenience and fast foods with natural, whole foods, you will have already eliminated the vast majority of food additives and colourings from your child's diet. Only a little additional vigilance will be required

to completely avoid these unnatural, chemical additives. Parents should get into the habit of reading nutrition labels on food packages, and decisively rejecting any foods that contain these colours or other additives.

Caffeine is another concern for children with attention disorders. Although in moderation the substance may cause no ill effects, it is a stimulant, causing an elevated 'high' feeling that is followed by a sudden low as energy is depleted. As a result, children with attention disorders may be particularly sensitive to its effects. Also, caffeinated drinks generally contain a great number of kilojoules, not to mention the food colouring, artificial sweeteners and other additives you are trying to avoid.

QUICK TIPS FOR PARENTS

- ✓ Remain open to the possibility of dietary influences on your child's behaviour.
- ✓ Provide your child a nutritionally sound diet of whole foods and home cooked meals.
- ✓ Avoid food colourings and other additives, such as tartrazine (102), Sunset Yellow (110), carmoisine (122), Ponceau 4R (124), and sodium benzoate (211).
- ✓ Avoid caffeine and excess sugar.
- ✓ Balance a good diet with plenty of activity time and exercise.
- ✓ Sufficient rest and sleep is also important.

USING A FOOD ELIMINATION PROGRAM

If you suspect a food allergy or food intolerance is causing medical complications or behavioural issues in your child, you will need to take steps to eliminate the culprit from your child's diet. Since it may be difficult to tell which foods are responsible, a food elimination program will be necessary in order to detect and weed out any potential problems.

The food elimination program consists of three stages, during which the child is put on a restrictive diet and certain foods are gradually reintroduced.

1. The first stage weeds out all potential problems from the child's diet. All junk foods are removed from your child's diet, and whole foods are restricted to the basics. Foods that commonly cause intolerance problems, such as dairy, whole grains, citrus fruits, and anything with additives, are also removed from your child's diet. This stage lasts 8 to 12 weeks, enabling you to monitor your child's behaviour closely, noting any changes.

2. The second stage involves the gradual reintroduction of foods that have been removed from the child's diet. Each food is reintroduced by itself, and the child's behaviour is monitored for several days before introducing another food. When a food is observed to

create a physical or behavioural problem, it can be permanently eliminated from your child's diet.

3. The third and final stage allows you to establish a long-term, whole food diet in accordance to your child's tolerances. Any foods that were identified as problematic in stage two can be completely eliminated. Although the nutritional plan that is reached in stage three may avoid certain foods, it should still be varied and nutritionally sound.

If you need help with a food elimination diet it is best to consult a nutritionist or your family doctor for assistance.

THE BENEFITS OF EXERCISE

A proper diet is not the only method that has been proven successful in treating physical and behavioural conditions. Exercise also carries many benefits for common childhood conditions.

✓ **Attention Disorders** – Physical activity helps to regulate brain functions. A healthy exercise regimen has been shown to increase the body's ability to focus and concentrate, which aids in the treatment of attention disorders.

✓ **Asthma** – Regular exercise strengthens the cardiovascular and respiratory systems, reducing the incidence of asthma attacks.

✓ **Anxiety** – Anxiety is caused by a reaction in the brain that causes fear and trepidation. Physical activity can help to regulate your child's brain function, and release body stress – reducing the frequency and severity of these attacks.

✓ **Depression and lethargy** – Regular exercise improves the body's appearance and physical condition, which in turn corresponds with improved self-esteem. Additionally, exercise releases mood-improving endorphins into the brain. Overall, a healthy exercise regimen can significantly reduce your child's depression or lethargy.

THE VALUE OF DIET AND EXERCISE AS A TREATMENT PLAN

Together with a departure from the values of healthy nutrition and exercise, our society has turned to a greater dependence on artificial substances. As food colourings and other additives are being used more and more in food production, the health of our children is deteriorating – yet many people fail to see the connection. Consequently, today more than ever, it is important to consider the role of diet in the manifestation of symptoms of childhood illness. Rather than using artificial drugs to combat the effects of artificial food additives, it's important to keep your mind open and explore other options.

5

A Plate for Life

The food basics: variety, smaller portion sizes, eating less sugar and fat

Quick Chapter Guide

✔ Understanding the elements of good nutrition
✔ What to eat: the five food groups
✔ Knowing how much to eat: paying attention to portion sizes
✔ Teaching your child to make healthy choices
✔ Handling a fussy eater
✔ Eating away from home and making good decisions
✔ Dealing with cravings
✔ Putting together your plan for healthy eating

A Plate for Life

The food basics: variety, smaller portion sizes, less sugar and less fat

Understanding the body's nutritional requirements and how food variety meets those needs is fundamental to healthy living and a balanced nutrition plan. Switching to healthier cooking methods, learning to read food labels, teaching good food choices and handling temptations is also important. It's easier than you think to include the main food groups as part of your daily eating plan - without labouring over complex meals or breaking the family grocery budget.

WHAT TO EAT: THE FIVE FOOD GROUPS

The human body has certain nutritional needs that must be met in order to maintain good health. Our body needs a sufficient supply of energy, and adequate amounts of the essential vitamins and nutrients for vitality and to function at peak performance.

Understanding good nutrition allows you to provide those right amounts. For every nutrient the body requires, there are numerous food choices able to satisfy our dietary needs, allowing for plenty of creativity and variety in planning family meals. However, in order to arrange food choices to fit seamlessly together into one meal, it's essential to have an understanding of the five food groups, what each one has to offer, and how to choose foods within those groups.

BREADS, CEREALS, RICE, PASTA AND NOODLES

The foundation of any diet should consist of grains, such as breads, breakfast cereals, rice, pasta, and noodles. These naturally low-fat foods provide carbohydrates – the body's main source of energy – dietary fibre, B vitamins, vitamin E, essential fatty acids, and many important minerals including iron, zinc, magnesium, and phosphorus. One of the primary dietary advantages of this food group is fibre, which helps keep our digestive system regular and is widely accepted as helping to reduce the risk of bowel cancer, coronary heart disease and diabetes.

Whole grains are far superior sources of fibre, minerals and vitamins compared to white grain based foods such as white breads and low-fibre cereals. It is relatively easy to substitute whole grains for white grains wherever possible; whole wheat and multi-grain bread, high-fibre breakfast cereals or muesli, brown rice, oatmeal, crisp breads, popcorn, and corn tortillas are all examples of whole grain foods.

Grain products with a lot of added sugar or fat – sugary breakfast cereals, cakes, biscuits, and pastries – are not included in this food group. The added kilojoules of these products far outweigh the nutritional value, making them suitable only as occasional treats.

Nutritional Benefits
✔ Dietary fibre
✔ Carbohydrates, the body's energy
✔ B and E vitamins
✔ Essential fatty acids
✔ Iron, zinc, magnesium and other essential minerals

Serving Sizes
• 2 slices of bread
• 1 medium bread roll
• 1 cup of porridge
• 1 cup of flaked cereal
• 1 cup of cooked rice or pasta or noodles
• ½ cup of muesli

Servings per Day
• Grain products are the staple of a healthy diet.
• Children and adults should have 5-6 servings each day.

QUICK TIPS FOR PARENTS
✔ Serve breads or wholegrain biscuits with each meal.
✔ Regularly use rice, pasta or noodles to accompany hot dishes.
✔ Eat high-fibre breakfast cereals or muesli daily.
✔ Include wholegrain cereals and pasta in soups and casseroles.
✔ Choose grain-based snacks such as low-fat cereal bars, muffins and popcorn.
✔ Substitute wholegrain for white-grain selections whenever possible.
✔ Avoid cereals and breads with added sugar and fat.

VEGETABLES

Vegetables are one of the most important sources of nutrients. Different vegetables contain carbohydrates, vitamins, and minerals in various quantities, making a wide variety of fresh vegetables an important part of a healthy diet. The dietary fibre, essential minerals, folate, vitamin C and other anti-oxidants in vegetables help to protect our bodies from many consequences of aging including high blood pressure, heart disease, and various forms of cancer.

Fresh vegetables are best; however frozen varieties and canned vegetables without added salt are also nutritious.

Nutritional Benefits
- ✓ Dietary fibre
- ✓ Vitamin A – found in dark orange and dark green vegetables like broccoli and spinach
- ✓ Vitamin C – plentiful in green vegetables such as cabbages and leafy greens
- ✓ Vitamin K – found in dark orange and dark green vegetables like broccoli and spinach
- ✓ Folate and other B Vitamins – found in dark green vegetables like broccoli and spinach, cauliflower, lentils and beans.
- ✓ Essential minerals including iron, potassium, and magnesium
- ✓ Carbohydrates

Servings per Day
- • Vegetables are an important source of many of the nutrients the body needs.
- • Children and adolescents should have 2-3 servings each day.
- • Adults should aim for 5 or more.
- • Pregnant or breastfeeding women should aim for 6+ servings a day.

Serving Size
- • ½ cup of vegetable juice
- • 1 medium potato or parsnip
- • ½ medium sweet potato
- • ½ cup cabbage, spinach, silverbeet, broccoli, cauliflower or brussels sprouts
- • 1 cup green leafy lettuce or salad vegetables
- • ½ cup broad beans, lentils, peas, green beans, zucchini, mushrooms, tomatoes, capsicum, cucumber, sweet corn, turnips, swede, sprouts, celery, eggplant

QUICK TIPS FOR PARENTS
- ✓ Serve a variety of fresh or frozen vegetables.
- ✓ Avoid frozen vegetables with special sauces.
- ✓ Avoid canned vegetables with high sodium content.
- ✓ Cook vegetables in a manner that preserves their nutritional value, and avoid cooking in butter, oils or fat.
- ✓ Try steaming, stir-frying, blanching and baking vegetables.
- ✓ Wherever possible add vegetables to casseroles, pastas, soups and other dishes.

FRUITS

Though not as nutrient-dense as vegetables, fruits are an important source of vitamins, minerals, natural sugars, dietary fibre and enzymes. As with vegetables, different fruits contain nutrients in differing quantities and for this reason a well balanced diet should include a variety of fruits. Fruit also contains naturally occurring antioxidants and phytonutrients that have been shown to have a positive effect on health.

Fresh fruit is the best choice; however stewed and canned fruits packed in juice can be substituted if fresh fruit is not available. Fruit juice, dried fruit, and canned fruit packed in syrup should be avoided, as these are higher in sugar and lower in nutritional value.

Nutritional Benefits

✓ Dietary fibre
✓ Vitamin A – contained in rockmelon, apricots, peaches, bananas, and nectarines
✓ Vitamin C – found in mangoes, papayas, melons, strawberries, kiwi fruit, and citrus fruits like oranges, mandarins, lemons and limes
✓ Other vitamins
✓ Minerals including potassium, calcium, magnesium, iron, and zinc
✓ Health-building antioxidants and phytonutrients
✓ Carbohydrates

Servings per Day

- Fruits are an important source of dietary fibre, essential nutrients and antioxidants.
- Most children and adults should have 2 servings of fruit every day.
- Teenagers and pregnant or breastfeeding women need 3+ servings a day.

Serving Size

- 1 medium-sized fruit e.g. apple, orange, mango, mandarin, banana, pear, peach
- 2 pieces of smaller fruit e.g. apricots, kiwi fruit, plums, figs
- 8-10 strawberries
- 15-20 grapes or cherries
- 1 cup of diced pieces or canned fruit
- ¼ medium melon (rockmelon, honeydew)
- 2 tablespoons sultanas
- ½ cup of fruit juice

QUICK TIPS FOR PARENTS

✓ Serve a variety of fruits to maximize nutritional intake.
✓ Opt for fresh, stewed, or canned fruit packed in juice.
✓ Arrange a fruit bowl at home for healthy snacks.
✓ Pack fruit for school lunches and work.
✓ Fruit like bananas, mandarins, and oranges that need to be peeled are best for avoiding pesticides – wash all other fruit thoroughly.
✓ Limit fruit juice and dried fruit.

MEAT, POULTRY, FISH, AND ALTERNATIVES (BEANS, EGGS, AND NUTS)

Meat and meat alternatives are the greatest source of protein – an essential nutrient the body needs for healthy tissue development and repair. Although red meat is the richest source of protein and other nutrients, poultry, pork, and fish are also good sources. Meat also contains valuable quantities of the B vitamins and is a particularly important source of vitamin B12, which is not found in plant foods, and is essential for the formation of red blood cells and the normal functioning of the nervous system.

Fish is also rich in Omega 3 fats, which are beneficial in reducing the risk of heart disease, alleviating symptoms associated with rheumatoid arthritis, and promoting the healthy development of brain tissue in babies.

Processed meats, such as hotdogs, sausage, pepperoni, bacon, ham and luncheon meats are typically high in fat and sodium, and relatively low in nutritional value. Therefore, they should be restricted items in your diet.

For vegetarians a number of foods can provide some of the key nutrients found in meats, fish and poultry, among them eggs, beans, tofu, nuts and some seeds. These foods are generally good sources of protein but have variable amounts of iron, zinc and vitamin B12. Some of these meat alternatives also have dietary concerns of their own, for example, egg yolks are extremely high in cholesterol.

Plant foods like lentils, black-eyed peas, chickpeas and other dried beans and peas are also inexpensive sources of protein. Unlike meats, beans are low in fat and high in fibre. Nuts and nut butters like peanuts and peanut butter are good sources of protein and iron; but they are higher in fat than other plant foods. Whole nuts are not suitable for young children because of potential problems with choking.

Nutritional Benefits

- ✓ Protein – found in highest quantities in red meat
- ✓ B12 vitamins – found in highest quantities in red meat, fish and eggs
- ✓ Essential minerals such as iron and zinc – found in highest quantities in red meat; somewhat lacking in beans, nuts and seeds
- ✓ Omega 3 fats – found in fish and other seafood
- ✓ Dietary fibre – plentiful in nuts and beans

Servings per Day

- Contrary to popular belief, people only need to eat 1 serving of meat or a meat alternative each day.
- Red meat should be eaten 3-4 times a week or replacement sources of iron will be needed; for girls, women, vegetarians, and athletes, this need is especially high.
- Fish should also be eaten every week as an essential source of Omega 3 fats.

Serving Size

- 65-100 grams of cooked meat or chicken (½ cup mince, 2 small chops, small chicken fillet, 2 slices of roast meat)
- ½ cup of cooked dried beans, lentils, chickpeas, split peas or canned beans
- 80-120 grams of cooked fish fillet
- 2 small eggs
- ⅔ of a cup of soybean curd (tofu)
- ⅓ of a cup of almonds or peanuts
- ¼ of a cup of sunflower or sesame seeds

For families aiming to lose weight it's important to realize that meat can also be high in fat. In order to limit fat intake as much as possible, you can take the following precautions whenever practical:

- ✓ Choose leaner cuts or trim off visible fat before cooking.
- ✓ Drain or skim off fat from cooked meats before using juices in stews, soups or gravies.
- ✓ Remove the skin from chicken for sandwiches, stir-fries and casseroles.
- ✓ Leave the skin on chicken while roasting to prevent it from getting too dry; then remove the skin before carving and serving the meat.

QUICK TIPS FOR PARENTS

- ✓ Serve 1 serving of meat or meat alternative each day.
- ✓ Serve red meat 3-4 times a week, or find a replacement source of iron.
- ✓ Include fish once a week as an importance source of Omega 3 fats.
- ✓ Reduce fat content of meat wherever possible.
- ✓ Limit consumption of processed meats.
- ✓ Limit consumption of egg yolks.
- ✓ Vegetarians need adequate replacement sources of iron and protein.
- ✓ NEVER give young children whole nuts.

DAIRY PRODUCTS (MILK, YOGHURT, AND CHEESE)

Dairy products are an important part of a balanced diet, providing the main source of calcium, the essential mineral necessary for the development and continued health of bones and teeth. Dairy products also provide protein, phosphorus, vitamins A and B, and zinc. Milk in particular contains just about every nutrient the human body needs.

However, dairy products are also a major source of the saturated fat in children's diets, requiring that children be given reduced fat and non-fat dairy products as they grow older.

- ✓ Children ages 0-2 require the extra energy from fat in milk and other dairy products. Therefore, during the first two years of life, children should be given full cream dairy products.
- ✓ Children ages 2-5 are gradually getting more of their energy requirements from carbohydrates. At this age, children can begin having reduced fat dairy products.
- ✓ Children ages 5 and older no longer need the fat in dairy products as an additional source of energy, and can be given skim milk.

For children who dislike milk, other ways of encouraging calcium consumption include offering calcium-fortified breakfast cereals; milk-based desserts like puddings, custards or yoghurts; adding skim-milk powder to mashed potatoes; sprinkling grated cheese on mashed potato, cauliflower, and other vegetables; and using cheese spread instead of butter or margarine spreads in sandwiches and on dry biscuits, savoury muffins and toast.

For lactose intolerant children parents should provide dairy substitutes like calcium enriched soy milk and soy yoghurts. Some varieties of cheddar and cottage cheeses have low lactose levels and may also be acceptable.

Nutritional Benefits
- ✓ Mineral calcium – most plentiful in milk
- ✓ Protein
- ✓ Vitamin A
- ✓ Vitamin B
- ✓ Phosphorus and zinc
- ✓ Bacteria that is beneficial to the body's digestive system – found in some yoghurts

Servings per Day
- Dairy or fortified dairy alternatives are essential for the body's calcium needs
- Adults and children should have 2 servings of dairy a day.
- Children aged 12-18 need 3 servings a day
- Women who are pregnant or breastfeeding, as well as adults 50 years or older, can benefit from 3 servings of dairy each day.

Serving Size
- 1 cup of milk
- 40g (2 slices) of cheese
- 1 cup custard
- 200g (1 small carton) of yoghurt
- 1 cup of calcium enriched soy milk*
- 5 sardines or ½ cup of pink salmon with bones*
- 1 cup of almonds*
- 1 cup of calcium-fortified cereal*
  *dairy alternatives

QUICK TIPS FOR PARENTS
- ✓ Children under 2 years should have full cream dairy products.
- ✓ Children 2+ and adults should have reduced fat dairy products.
- ✓ Skim milk is acceptable for children ages 5 and older.
- ✓ For fussy eaters try healthy shakes, yoghurts, custards, cheese spreads, and grating cheeses into pasta, rice, and other hot dishes.
- ✓ Lactose intolerant children should try non-dairy soy replacements and dairy products with low levels of lactose like cheddar cheese.

Reading food labels and checking ingredients will often highlight hidden fats and sugars. Of course, it is best to buy natural whole foods whenever possible; making meals from scratch allows you to have complete control over what goes into your family's food. It's also important to remember that sweets and fats are a normal part of any diet so long as they are eaten in moderation; you don't have to cut them out completely.

Moderating Sugary Sweets and Snacks: What Do I Tell My Kids?

For children who regularly eat sugary treats and snacks suddenly being denied these foods may seem bewildering. Parents are bound to hear demands of, "But why?" Rather than brushing aside these questions, tell your child the truth. Explain the concepts of good and bad nutrition as simply as possible for younger children, and describe why the desired food is not good for them.

Although your child will probably be confused at first, you can make the concept of nutrition easier to understand by involving them in grocery shopping and label reading, meal planning and preparation. Most children are by nature curious and eager to learn, and they are bound to take interest in the family's nutrition if you make them feel involved.

WHAT NOT TO EAT: CUTTING OUT SWEETS AND FATS

It is no secret that moderating the amount of sweets and fats we eat is important. Sweets are usually packed with refined sugar and have very little nutritional value. Fats, especially saturated fats, are associated with many diseases and an increase in body fat. Most people can spot sweets and even most fats easily in their everyday foods. The problem comes from the hidden fats and sugars.

A cut of steak with the fat left on is easy to spot. Everyone knows that full cream milk contains a great deal of fat. Chocolate, soft drink, cakes, pies and other treats contain lots of sugar. It is easy to limit a child's intake of these foods and explain why. It becomes a little trickier with some foods that have hidden fat or sugar. For example, many food manufacturers making low-fat foods replace the fat with more sugar to preserve the taste. The fat content of the food goes down but the overall energy content does not. So for many people consciously trying to lose weight through better food choices - accepting food marketing claims on face value - means they are still buying energy-dense or fattening foods without intending to.

QUICK TIPS FOR PARENTS

- ✓ Read food labels to find hidden sugars and fats.
- ✓ Explain healthy food choices to your child.
- ✓ Involve your child in grocery shopping, meal planning, and meal preparation.
- ✓ Look for healthier alternatives to traditional treats and snacks.
- ✓ Sugary treats and snacks are still ok in moderation.

THE IMPORTANCE OF FOOD VARIETY

Another important component of a sound nutritional plan is food variety - it is important to spread the food groups out across the daily meals. Including a variety of foods from each food group ensures that you will not become bored. Variety will also give you sufficient choice to ensure you can find something healthy to satisfy your desires for poorer food choices from the past.

Maintaining variety in your diet isn't just to keep things interesting: it also serves an important physiological purpose. Because different food digests at different rates, the body prefers food variety during the digestive process. By balancing the quick-digesting carbohydrates in fruits and vegetables with the slower fats and proteins in meats our bodies are able to maintain optimum energy levels to sustain activity and function while continuing digestion. Additionally, different foods offer different nutrients, so variety ensures that we absorb all the essential nutrients needed throughout the day by combining various foods during meal times.

Food variety choices are only limited by the imagination. The key with variety is to make sure that all of the food groups are represented, and the recommended servings are being reached. To ensure this happens, plan your day's meals and snacks ahead of time, and double check that all food groups are represented in main meals.

The Ideal Plate

The ideal plate should be balanced with food variety from the different food groups including meat, carbohydrates like rice, pasta or noodles, and salad or vegetables in proportions similar to those illustrated here. Moderate portion sizes; add bread and a glass of water to complement, and a little fresh fruit to finish.

> **"It is very important not to pressure your child to clean his or her plate. Kids know when they are no longer hungry, and forcing them to continue eating after that point teaches them to overeat."**

KNOWING HOW MUCH TO EAT: PAYING ATTENTION TO PORTION SIZES

Another factor in healthy eating is portion size. Current culture has a tendency to super-size everything; even non-fast food restaurants are offering larger portions in order to attract customers. Convenience foods have jumped on the bandwagon, as well. In this environment, it is more important than ever to be conscious of appropriate portion sizes.

Leaving a meal feeling full is usually a sign that portion sizes were too large. That's not to say that you should leave a meal feeling hungry; appropriately sized portions should be enough to satisfy without leaving you feeling full or uncomfortable.

Appropriate portion sizes should be based on recommended servings and serving sizes. However, keep in mind that portion sizes are also dependent on the type of food and its energy content; for example, portion size is less rigid for a leafy green salad with light dressing, but more important for energy-dense foods, such as steak.

An easy way to accustom yourself to smaller portion sizes is to eat considerably smaller meals, but to schedule them more frequently; not only will this help you adjust to getting less food, but it is also healthier, as more frequent meals and snacks allow your metabolism to maintain a constant rate.

It is very important not to pressure your child to clean his or her plate. Kids know when they are no longer hungry, and forcing them to continue eating after that point teaches them to overeat.

QUICK TIPS FOR PARENTS

- ✓ Base portion size on recommended servings and serving suggestions.
- ✓ Eat smaller, more frequent meals when possible.
- ✓ Don't pressure your child to clean his or her plate.
- ✓ Sugary or fatty foods, when eaten at all, should be eaten in smaller portions than other foods.
- ✓ Be wary of portion sizes when eating out.

EATING AWAY FROM HOME AND MAKING GOOD DECISIONS

Although home cooked meals are by far the best way to control the ingredients and provide a balanced diet for your family, the reality is that it just isn't always possible. Adults and kids alike have busier schedules these days, making family meals less frequent and harder to plan. And then there are school lunches, which provide children with greater freedom to choose what they eat and don't eat, possibly disrupting your carefully planned balanced diet. This doesn't mean that your plan for a healthier lifestyle should be abandoned, however - there are plenty of ways in which you and your family can eat healthily away from home.

Eating out often brings its own pressures to overeat. To avoid feeling that you must eat a lot of food when you eat out, try half orders when they are available, entrée sizes and sides, or split your order with another family member. Don't be afraid to ask for a take away container or doggy bag if the meals are too large to finish, or you over order. Wherever possible choose meals that are healthy, offer a selection from the main food groups and are cooked in a manner that does not add excess fat or sugar.

Eating out is usually a bigger concern for children, as most kids' menus are not very healthy. Some restaurants may be able to substitute a half order of an adult menu item, or your children could share a healthy adult meal or have an entree. If the restaurant serves larger-than-necessary portion sizes, try splitting an adult meal with your child.

Eating lunch at school can be another concern for maintaining your child's healthy diet. Whether you pack a lunch for your child or allow them to buy food at school, you have basically the same issue: how to ensure that your child is getting healthy meals away from home. Children frequently trade parts of their lunches, and unless you make your child's lunch interesting, the healthier selections will often be the first to go. To reduce the chance of trading a healthy lunch for junk food, make sure that it is filled with foods your child enjoys – and remember to vary what you give them so they don't become bored.

It's also a great motivator to involve your child in helping you pack their lunch the night before, giving parents an opportunity to turn the chore into a learning experience by teaching their kids the nutritional value of each item in their lunch pack. If your child buys food at school, be sure to ask them about lunch in routine conversation about their day - poor food choices can often be corrected with a little extra encouragement.

QUICK TIPS FOR PARENTS

- ✓ Learn to ask questions about how menu items are prepared or make special requests to increase the nutritional value of a menu item.
- ✓ Choose entrée size adult meals or share with children rather than relying upon kids' menu items.
- ✓ Grilled, stir-fried, baked, and steamed meals that offer a selection from the major food groups are best.
- ✓ Share desserts and avoid sugary drinks with meals.
- ✓ Pack healthy lunches that your child will like.
- ✓ Teach your child to make healthy food choices away from home.
- ✓ Remember the importance of variety.

TEACHING YOUR CHILD TO MAKE HEALTHY CHOICES

Planning healthy meals for your family is a great way to improve your child's health; however, you may realize that fostering healthy lifelong habits in your child will take more than simply a nutritious meal plan. And, since your child is one of the biggest reasons for undertaking this shift to healthier eating, it makes sense to make sure your child is prepared to make healthy decisions.

Children are driven primarily by impulse; food manufacturers know this and take advantage of it by creating treats that taste good, yet are exceedingly low in nutritional value. Most kids will not understand or make better decisions on their own - at least not without being taught to do so. Although kids can be taught what a healthy diet entails through modelling and involvement in food decisions and preparation, the initiative to eat better must come from the parents.

Modelling is one of the best ways to teach children a desired behaviour. If you have any doubts, think about the many times your child has said and done what they've seen you do, despite your best efforts to teach them otherwise. In other words, if you gripe about your veggies and won't touch certain kinds, your child will follow suit; but if you model eating – and enjoying – a variety of vegetables, your child will likely never think twice about doing the same.

Children also learn from doing. The best way to take advantage of this is to involve your child in every aspect of your healthy diet: everything from grocery shopping and making decisions on which products to buy, to meal planning and preparation. Children are naturally curious and will learn without even realizing it, so long as they are involved and interested. Explaining to your child your reasoning behind certain food choices and how to read and understand nutrition labels will teach them to apply concepts such as healthy, unhealthy, natural, and processed.

Encouraging kids to help plan and prepare meals makes their involvement more fun, and gives even further opportunities for you to teach healthy habits.

QUICK TIPS FOR PARENTS

✓ Teach children about healthy choices, and how to make them.

✓ Lead by example to reinforce healthy choices and behaviours.

✓ Involve your child in the decision-making process, everything from shopping and putting away groceries, to meal planning and preparation.

✓ Encourage your child to use their creativity in planning and preparing meals.

✓ Most importantly, make it fun!

HANDLING A FUSSY EATER

There is nothing more frustrating for a parent than a fussy eater. Children who refuse to eat anything except cheese on toast and plain pasta can make implementing a balanced diet very difficult. However, before you can find a solution you must understand the problem. Fussy eaters are really just inexperienced eaters. It is also important to note that most picky children do not grow up to be picky adults. Therefore, you needn't feel pressured to change your fussy eater overnight.

The best solution is to provide an atmosphere of healthy eating that promotes food experimentation and variety. This can be fostered in many different ways:

✓ Don't pressure your child to try new foods. Simply placing the new food on their plate is enough. However, it may take some time before they may be willing to try it: studies show that children must be faced with a food as many as 20 times, without pressure, before they feel comfortable enough to try it.

✓ Make a game out of eating by encouraging your child to eat different colours. This works particularly well with young children, who are often very eager to show off their new skills in identification and naming games.

✓ Don't make mealtime a big production. Instead, simply put the food on the table and start eating. It may be

tempting to nag your child to eat all of their vegetables or finish a glass of milk, but this only draws attention to the fact that they might not like certain food items, or foster deliberate rebellion.

✓ Always offer at least one food that's a favourite. However, do not allow kids to fill up on this alone and ignore other foods they may find less appetizing. Remind them that there are other foods available with the meal, but again, refrain from nagging.

✓ Use mealtimes as an opportunity to discuss the health benefits of the different foods on your child's plate. Challenge kids by asking them to recall nutrition information you have explained in the past.

✓ Surprise your child by disguising a healthy meal as one of their favourites. Substituting a few ingredients can often totally transform the nutritional value of a meal. Wait until your child is eating to explain, positively, the changes you made and how it makes the meal better.

✓ Try eating somewhere other than the dinner table, for example in your child's cubby house, or picnic style on a blanket in the lounge room.

Again, it's important not to pressure your child. Allowing kids to eat what they like, as long as it is healthy, is not going to do permanent damage. Fussy eaters are likely to grow out this stage, as long as you maintain an atmosphere of healthy eating and variety.

DEALING WITH CRAVINGS

The fear of cravings can be one of the most intimidating parts of changing one's diet. However, it's important to remember that a balanced diet isn't a prison term. The key to dealing with cravings – without breaking your family's healthy eating plan – is to indulge when you get a craving, but in moderation. Watch your portion sizes, and make choices that are healthier than past favourites.

Allowing your child to give in to cravings occasionally also teaches an important lesson. Children are driven by impulses, but allowing them to indulge occasionally and in small amounts teaches them how to control their impulses. It is important for a child to know when to stop eating, no matter how good it tastes – just as it is important for kids to know the difference between indulging in an occasional treat, and eating it all the time.

The good news is that cravings won't happen as often as you fear. The fruits you eat on a daily basis should generally satisfy your sweet tooth, and spiced and flavourful foods keep meals interesting. Maintaining an interesting and tasteful variety of healthy food choices prevents from feeling that you're being denied anything. Healthy eating should not be about boring, bland meals, but about natural, flavoursome, and healthy choices that both delight the palate and satisfy the body's needs for nutrients.

QUICK TIPS FOR PARENTS

- ✓ Remember: fussy eaters are really just inexperienced eaters.
- ✓ Its important to be patient, flexible and not pressure fussy eaters.
- ✓ Don't feel intimidated by cravings - allow yourself and your family to indulge occasionally.
- ✓ Teach your child how much indulgence is appropriate.
- ✓ Guide your child through the process of learning impulse control.
- ✓ Experiment with healthier alternatives to sweets and snacks.

PUTTING TOGETHER YOUR PLAN FOR HEALTHY EATING

A healthy, balanced diet is an important foundation for a healthy, happy life. By changing your family's diet, you're not just helping family members to lose weight or children to develop properly: you're fostering healthy habits that will increase every family member's quality of life.

The prospect of change may seem a little overwhelming. Between food groups, food preparation methods, and strategies for dealing with fussy eaters; you may not know where to start. But as long as you can follow the basic guidelines, you and your family will be well on your way to better nutrition and health.

The Foundation of Your Healthy Eating Plan

- ✓ Introduce dietary changes slowly, rather than all at once.
- ✓ Plan meals that include a variety of foods.
- ✓ Ensure that all food groups are represented.
- ✓ Avoid excess sweets and fats.
- ✓ Choose healthy methods of preparing and cooking food.
- ✓ Be mindful of portion sizes.
- ✓ Choose smaller more frequent meals throughout the day rather than the traditional 3 meal plan.
- ✓ Find healthy ways to make your meals taste good.
- ✓ Model healthy eating habits for your children.
- ✓ Involve your child in making decisions on and preparing meals.
- ✓ Resist the urge to pressure your child to try new foods or clean their plate.
- ✓ Find replacement sources of nutrients for foods your child can't - or won't - eat.
- ✓ Make healthy decisions when eating away from home, and teach your child to do the same.
- ✓ Indulge cravings occasionally.
- ✓ Make food planning and preparation a family affair.

6

Better Beverages

Juggling water, milk, juices and soft drinks

Quick Chapter Guide

- ✔ The importance of healthy beverages as part of a balanced nutrition plan
- ✔ Why poor beverage choice can load the body with excess sugars and additives
- ✔ Water: the mystery fluid that makes up two-thirds of your body
- ✔ Milk for children of different ages: juggling whole, low-fat and skim varieties
- ✔ Fruit juice: all the vitamins of real fruit without the benefits of fibre
- ✔ Soft drinks, mixes, and other sweetened drinks
- ✔ Including beverages and dental care in your healthy lifestyle

Better Beverages

Juggling water, milk, juices and soft drinks

A variety of healthy beverages throughout the day are an integral part of a healthy diet, but all too often people forget to include beverages in their daily nutrition plan. As a result, they overlook an important part of their diet that has the potential to either boost their goal of improving the health of the entire family, or sabotage these plans. When selected using the same principles that guide a balanced diet, beverages can maintain the body's hydration, provide valuable nutrients and facilitate proper digestion. On the flip side, if a healthy balance between beverage choices is not met, the fluids we put into our body can be disastrous to a healthy diet, loading the body up on excess sugars and additives, and causing dehydration and nutrient loss.

BEVERAGES AND NUTRITION

Water

What if you were told that there was one perfect fluid for hydrating the body? This mystery fluid makes up two-thirds of your body; drinking plenty of it each day ensures a smoothly functioning digestive system, yet doesn't add any sugar, fat, or kilojoules to your diet. If you didn't know any better, it might come as a surprise to you to know that this elixir of life is yours – on tap!

Even though most people know that water is their best bet for staying hydrated, all too often they pass it up for coffee, tea, or soft drink. However, relying on drinks other than water ultimately leads to dehydration – a condition that means more than just a dry throat or parched lips. Depending on the extent, dehydration causes a variety of symptoms including fatigue, headaches, irritability, respiratory problems, and impaired temperature regulation. For those aiming to lose those extra kilos, dehydration also decreases metabolism, meaning that the body burns energy more slowly.

The key to staying hydrated is to add regular water intake throughout the day in addition to food and other beverages. Most people should drink between 6-8 glasses of water a day. Importantly, hydration needs increase with physical activity by about a glass every 30-45 minutes. This does not include other beverages, even, for example, sports drinks – only water can truly satisfy your body's need for hydration.

Unfortunately, with the availability of other, more interesting drinks, water faces a unique problem these days: many people, children especially, don't want to drink it. Although it may be tempting to add a drink mix or flavouring to water to encourage kids to drink it, this changes water by adding sugars, preservatives and other additives. Instead, keep water in the fridge at all times and limit other choices. If your kids need flavour to make the change to water, mix in a little of their favourite fruit juice or add slices of lemon or orange to make water more appealing.

Always remember that there are no replacements for water in a healthy diet. Modelling good hydrating habits for your children can help encourage them to drink more water. You should also explain to your child why we drink water, and the importance of staying hydrated and avoiding soft drink and other sugary beverages.

For school aged children, it's always a good idea to buy them a drink bottle they like. Cool drink bottles disguise water and allow kids to hydrate wherever they are, without succumbing to pressures from their peers about uncool drink choices.

QUICK TIPS FOR PARENTS

- ✓ Drink 6-8 glass of water a day, and encourage your child to do the same.
- ✓ Add an extra glass of water for every 30-45 minutes of physical activity.
- ✓ Keep water in the refrigerator.
- ✓ Dilute water with a little fruit juice or add cut citrus fruits if necessary.
- ✓ Limit other beverage choices.
- ✓ Model good hydrating habits and explain to your child the benefits of water.
- ✓ Buy kids cool drink bottles for school and sports to encourage regular hydration and help avoid peer pressures.

Milk

Milk is a controversial beverage, as many nutritionists disagree about how much of it one can or should drink. On one hand, milk is a terrific source of calcium, protein, and vitamins; but on the other hand, it is also high in fat.

However, there are some guidelines that you and your family should follow. Almost every nutritionist agrees that during the first 2 years of a child's life, full cream milk should be served in order to provide the growing child with plenty of energy. Between the ages of 2 and 5, children can be given reduced fat milk, as they are beginning to get much more of their energy from other foods; however, they still depend on getting a little fat for energy. Skim milk becomes a healthy alternative for children at 5 years of age.

For the most part, adults and children aged 1-11 should have a maximum of 2 glasses of milk a day; more than that may cause excess fat intake, eventually leading to weight gain. (Note that 2 glasses would fulfil the daily requirements for dairy.) However, adolescents aged 12-18 (who are growing rapidly), women who are pregnant or breastfeeding, and adults over 50 years can benefit from up to 3 glasses of milk a day. (For these people, 3 glasses would fulfil the daily requirements for dairy.)

Unfortunately, some children do not take well to milk, either because they dislike the taste or because they are lactose

"When selecting fruit juice make sure to avoid those loaded with extra sugar or preservatives. A juicer or other natural extraction method is great for making fresh, healthy juices at home."

Juice

Fruit juice is a beverage that is overrated and overused in modern society. Juice manufacturers routinely tout the nutritional benefits of their products, yet they neglect to mention the mind-boggling amount of added sugar in their drinks. In other words, select products according to what the nutrition labels say, rather than what the product's advertising says.

Many juice manufacturers claim that their products are 100% juice. However, that doesn't necessarily mean that they don't have added sugar. Checking the ingredient list will tell you right away whether this is the case. Be sure to avoid any juice that contains food colourings or preservatives.

And although quality juice brands contain most of the nutrients that fruit does, remember that one of the most important nutritional elements – dietary fibre – is missing.

For these reasons, juice can be a good treat and does contain some of the essential nutrients. It is a simple way to get one of the fruit servings for the day. However too much juice can be a detriment to any weight loss plan and should not be seen as a replacement for whole fruit. A small glass of juice, preferably diluted with 50% water, with breakfast should be enough to satisfy the craving for sweets and give needed nutrients. When selecting fruit juice make sure to avoid those loaded with extra sugar or preservatives. A juicer or other natural extraction method is great for making fresh, healthy juices at home.

intolerant. Incentives such as chocolate milk can encourage fussy eaters to drink enough milk, but must be used in moderation, as they contribute excess sugar in the diet. For children who simply can't have milk, alternatives such as soy milk are available; however, these alternatives are also frequently energy-dense, and will need to be taken into account when planning your child's diet.

QUICK TIPS FOR PARENTS

- ✓ Give children aged 0-2 full cream milk.
- ✓ Give children aged 2-5 reduced fat milk.
- ✓ Give children over 5 years reduced fat or skim milk.
- ✓ Serve adults and children aged 1-11 up to 2 glasses of milk a day.
- ✓ Serve adolescents aged 12-18 up to 3 glasses of milk a day.
- ✓ If you are pregnant, breastfeeding, or over 50, you can benefit from up to 3 glasses of milk a day.
- ✓ Use incentives such as chocolate milk in moderation.
- ✓ Provide alternatives for children with lactose intolerance.

Another alternative is vegetable juice. These juices generally don't have the same sweet taste or added sugar of fruit juice, but they are packed with vitamins and minerals. As always, it is important to read the product's nutritional information before making a purchase. Vegetable juice can provide an easy way to get one of the daily vegetable servings in, but without the added benefits of fibre.

QUICK TIPS FOR PARENTS

✓ Read nutrition labels.
✓ Avoid juice with food colourings or preservatives in the ingredients list.
✓ Serve no more than 1 glass of juice a day.
✓ Dilute juice with 1 equal part of water.
✓ Try vegetables juices for an easy vegetable serving without the high sugar content.

Soft Drinks, Mixes, and Other Sweetened Drinks

Soft drinks and other sweetened drinks clearly constitute a thriving industry. Despite the fact that they have little or no nutritional value, and loads of excess sugar, soft drinks are a favourite of children and teens.

Soft drinks are not only energy-dense and full of additives, but they also leach the body of necessary nutrients - leading to problems such as weight gain, blood sugar problems, and nutrient imbalances. And although diet soft drinks may appear to circumvent the problems associated with excess sugar, the artificial sweeteners, food colourings, and other additives are just as bad for the body – if not worse.

Some non-carbonated alternatives boast additional nutritional value; however, be aware that it doesn't make them any better for your child. No matter how much vitamin C or other nutrients they claim to contain, they are still packed with sugar, with the same potential for excess weight gain and reactions to artificial additives.

Caffeine is a common additive in cola-type soft drinks and energy drinks. Many studies suggest that caffeine may cause problems associated with anxiety, concentration, weight loss and dehydration in children and adults. The main dietary source of caffeine for children aged 2–12 years is most commonly cola-type soft drinks; in adolescents and teens it is coffee, tea, energy drinks and cola drinks. Children should be discouraged from drinking beverages containing caffeine, while teens should use caution and moderation. Where possible, low-caffeine, caffeine-free, and low-sugar varieties are recommended.

If a sweet drink is absolutely necessary, natural fruit juice should always be chosen over a soft drink. However, as you will not always be available to make this decision for your child, it is important to talk to them about the reasons why soft drinks are detrimental to their health.

BEVERAGES AND DENTAL CARE

Good nutrition benefits your family's overall health in a number of ways; one of these is the lower incidence of dental problems. Poor beverage choice in particular can have an adverse effect on dental health, through a combination of accelerated tooth decay and leaching of valuable nutrients, including calcium.

There are a number of precautions you and your family can take to protect your teeth. For instance, the impact of sugary beverages on your children's teeth can be lessened by having them sip sugary drinks through a straw, and by requiring that they brush their teeth immediately after enjoying a sugary food or beverage.

Diet can also aid your toothbrush in keeping your teeth clean. Plan meals with a variety of foods, both crunchy and soft. Crunchy fruits and vegetables help clean the teeth by scraping off tartar and deposits.

Another habit to get into is preventing your baby or toddler from sleeping with a bottle, as this keeps the beverage in their mouth for longer, which will cause accelerated tooth decay.

Water is also important to dental health. Tap water usually has fluoride in it, which helps keep teeth healthy and strong. If your tap water does not have sufficient levels of fluoride, or your family drink bottled water, you may need to provide a fluoride supplement for your child.

Of course, the foundation of oral health is regular brushing and flossing. Start fostering these values early in your child's life, gradually teaching them to brush and floss. It is also important to schedule dental visits every 6 months to a year; this allows your dentist to catch problems when they are small, and help correct them before they get out of hand.

QUICK TIPS FOR PARENTS

✓ Limit intake of sugary foods.
✓ Drink sugary beverages through a straw.
✓ Serve a variety of crunchy foods that will help clean the teeth.
✓ Avoid letting infants and toddlers sleep with a bottle.
✓ Provide fluoride supplements when tap or bottled water is not a sufficient source.
✓ Foster regular brushing and flossing habits.
✓ Schedule regular dentist appointments.

7

Mind your Ps & Qs!

Understanding food marketing and labels

Quick Chapter Guide

✔ Know the difference between marketing and informing
✔ Consider the hidden meaning of nutrition claims and slogans
✔ Understanding and using the nutritional information panel
✔ The ingredients list - another important feature of food packaging
✔ Food additives: knowing what to look for
✔ Unwrapping other components of food labels
✔ Reading food labels for a healthy diet

Mind Your Ps and Qs!

Understanding food marketing and labels

Understanding basic nutrition and applying it to a healthy eating plan is really not that hard. The most difficult part is determining what foods fit that new lifestyle. This isn't hard when selecting fresh fruits and vegetables, breads and lean cuts of meat and fish. The challenge comes when buying packaged products and having to decipher food marketing claims and nutritional labels to make good food choices. Sorting out the details on food packaging takes a little understanding of what is required on labels, but is well worth the effort.

THE BIG BUSINESS OF FOOD MARKETING

The food industry has grown exponentially during recent decades, and competition between food manufacturers has increased. The abundance of brands available for consumers to choose from puts manufacturers under a great deal of pressure to market their products memorably.

Exaggerated claims and health promises, vitamin and mineral fortification or enrichment, endorsements from TV and sports personalities, toys and cartoon characters that target younger audiences - these are just a few of the ways food and beverage marketing professionals work to sell their products.

It is no coincidence that the foods eaten most frequently are also the same foods that are featured regularly in mass marketing campaigns. Children are eating less fresh fruits and vegetables and more chocolate, soft drink, sugary cereals, and fast foods. Media companies use child psychologists, focus groups, and target audience studies to find the best methods of getting and keeping your child's attention long enough to get the message across. These methods are then used to market high sugar, high fat, low nutrient foods.

Children and teens need to be educated to understand food marketing and what a healthy food choice is. Being informed consumers is the best defence against big business marketing campaigns. Kids can be taught to read labels just like adults. Start out with simple kilojoule and sugar content recognition and as they get older teach them the significance of the other nutrients listed.

To counter the push to educate consumers against marketing tricks, many companies add a few vitamins and minerals to otherwise low value foods to attract conscientious parents. With claims for vitamin enriched content and more minerals splashed across the front of the package manufacturers are hoping consumers won't turn the package around and look into the actual content. Throwing some vitamin C into a puffed corn ball with artificial colours and flavours, along with nearly 100% sugar content, does not make it a healthy choice.

Studies have shown that simple name and/or package recognition leads to more impulse buying than most people believe. Children are especially susceptible because they are less conscious of the health side of foods and are more motivated by media influences. Advertising can play a big role in food selection. Unfortunately, until the media sources, government agencies, and food manufacturers come to some sort of agreement the advertisements will continue. The important thing to remember with food marketing is not to believe the claims - check the foods out by reading the labels carefully.

UNWRAPPING FOOD PACKAGING CLAIMS

In order to help consumers make educated decisions, Food Standards Australia New Zealand (FSANZ) requires that all food manufacturers include specific nutritional information on each product. The nutritional claims that food manufacturers can make are also regulated by FSANZ guidelines. Claims are statements and slogans on the packaging related to nutritional content of a food or health-related benefits.

Nutritional content claims may include for example;

✓ **No Added Sugar:** the product does not have added sugar; however, it may contain any amount of natural sugars.

✓ **Reduced Fat/Reduced Salt:** the product has at least a 25% reduction from the original product.

✓ **Low-fat:** solid foods must contain less than 3% fat; and liquid foods must contain less than 1.5% fat.

✓ **Fat Free:** the product must contain less than 0.15% fat.

✓ **High in Calcium:** the product contains beneficial amounts of calcium with reference to daily recommended intake.

Food marketing claims, the nutritional information panel, ingredients list and other information all have a place on food packaging. The cereal box below is a good example of how this information is usually presented or marketed:

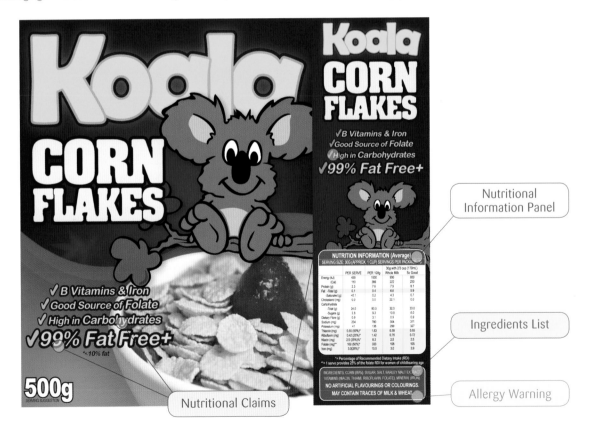

Health-related claims may include statements like 'calcium is good for strong bones and teeth'; and 'helps keep you regular as part of a high-fibre diet.' Health-related claims need to be substantiated by scientific evidence. However, it's important to realize that many food manufacturers use nutrition-based marketing to sell their products and, even though the FSANZ regulates how manufacturers advertise these health benefits, food manufacturers can – and do – manipulate their marketing campaigns to make their products seem more beneficial than they actually are. Here are some common examples of misleading claims:

✓ **Lite/Light:** may refer to the texture, colour, or taste of the product rather than the fat or energy content.

✓ **93% Fat Free:** sounds healthy but the product contains 7% fat which is not particularly good.

✓ **No Cholesterol/Low Cholesterol/Cholesterol Free:** again sounds healthy but the product may still contain significant amounts of fat.

✓ **Baked Not Fried:** the product may still contain significant amounts of fat.

✓ **100% Fruit:** the product may have 100% fruit but may also have added sugar; the combination of fruit may vary from what is shown on the label.

Because food manufacturers are so skilled at marketing their products, shoppers need to be well educated as to what nutritional information really constitutes a healthy food selection. Again it is better to ignore the claims, and rely on the nutritional information panel and the ingredients list to really decipher the value of packaged food.

UNDERSTANDING THE NUTRITIONAL INFORMATION PANEL

Nutritional information panels on manufactured foods enable consumers to see what they are buying. There are some exceptions, such as very small packages, herbs and spices, coffee and tea, and single ingredient foods; however, most products that you find in the grocery store should have a clearly visible panel that details the nutritional content.

Information on the nutritional information panel includes details that are important for making a healthy food selection, including:

✓ the number of servings of the food in the package
✓ the average serving size, expressed in grams or millilitres
✓ the average energy content, expressed in kilojoules, in a serving and per 100g of the food
✓ the amount of protein, fat, saturated fat, carbohydrate, sodium and sugars, in a serving and per 100g of the food
✓ the name and quantity of any other nutrient of which a nutrition claim is made.

The Nutritional Information Panel also specifies how much of the fat content is saturated fat, and how much of the carbohydrates are sugars, giving a better idea of the impact a product could have on your family's weight or health issues such as blood cholesterol.

And for people wanting to lose weight, it's particularly important to understand the two ratings for the amount of nutrients included in a product: the amount per serving size, and the amount per 100g or 100ml.

✓ The amount per serving size allows you to calculate your family's consumption of certain nutrients and energy for the average portion size, whereas
✓ The amount per 100g gives a number that can be used to compare similar products with different serving sizes, for example two brands of yoghurt packaged in slightly different container sizes.

This information is intended to inform the consumer about the nutritional value of the food contained in the packaging. Any claims made about the nutrient content of a food must be expressed on the label as well. For example, a food that claims to be high in vitamin C must include the amount of vitamin C in each serving and per 100g of the food.

Below is an example of the nutritional information panel found on most packages:

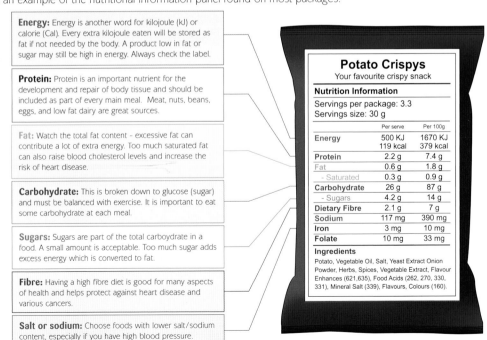

Energy: Energy is another word for kilojoule (kJ) or calorie (Cal). Every extra kilojoule eaten will be stored as fat if not needed by the body. A product low in fat or sugar may still be high in energy. Always check the label.

Protein: Protein is an important nutrient for the development and repair of body tissue and should be included as part of every main meal. Meat, nuts, beans, eggs, and low fat dairy are great sources.

Fat: Watch the total fat content - excessive fat can contribute a lot of extra energy. Too much saturated fat can also raise blood cholesterol levels and increase the risk of heart disease.

Carbohydrate: This is broken down to glucose (sugar) and must be balanced with exercise. It is important to eat some carbohydrate at each meal.

Sugars: Sugars are part of the total carboydrate in a food. A small amount is acceptable. Too much sugar adds excess energy which is converted to fat.

Fibre: Having a high fibre diet is good for many aspects of health and helps protect against heart disease and various cancers.

Salt or sodium: Choose foods with lower salt/sodium content, especially if you have high blood pressure.

Potato Crispys
Your favourite crispy snack

Nutrition Information

Servings per package: 3.3
Servings size: 30 g

	Per serve	Per 100g
Energy	500 KJ 119 kcal	1670 KJ 379 kcal
Protein	2.2 g	7.4 g
Fat	0.6 g	1.8 g
- Saturated	0.3 g	0.9 g
Carbohydrate	26 g	87 g
- Sugars	4.2 g	14 g
Dietary Fibre	2.1 g	7 g
Sodium	117 mg	390 mg
Iron	3 mg	10 mg
Folate	10 mg	33 mg

Ingredients

Potato, Vegetable Oil, Salt, Yeast Extract Onion Powder, Herbs, Spices, Vegetable Extract, Flavour Enhances (621,635), Food Acids (262, 270, 330, 331), Mineral Salt (339), Flavours, Colours (160).

"If you or someone in your family suffers from a food allergy or intolerance, the ingredients list is especially helpful, as it allows you to determine whether or not the product contains the problem food."

Compare the energy, fat and calcium content per 100ml serve for the different varieties of milk below. All provide beneficial amounts of calcium; however you will notice a substantial difference in energy and fat between the full cream, low-fat and skim varieties:

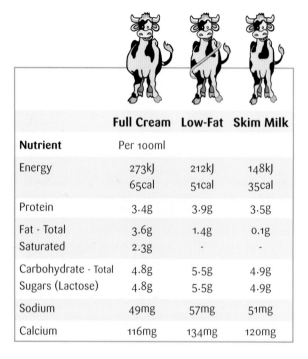

Nutrient	Full Cream	Low-Fat	Skim Milk
	Per 100ml		
Energy	273kJ	212kJ	148kJ
	65cal	51cal	35cal
Protein	3.4g	3.9g	3.5g
Fat - Total	3.6g	1.4g	0.1g
Saturated	2.3g	-	-
Carbohydrate - Total	4.8g	5.5g	4.9g
Sugars (Lactose)	4.8g	5.5g	4.9g
Sodium	49mg	57mg	51mg
Calcium	116mg	134mg	120mg

Importantly, when using the serving size to calculate your daily intake, remember to recalculate the nutritional or energy content whenever you serve portions that are larger or smaller than the serving size listed on the label. For example, an average-sized tin of soup may list 2.5 servings in the can. Most people, when eating soup, eat the whole can. So, to get an accurate count of kilojoules, proteins, fats, carbohydrates, and sodium you must multiply each quantity listed under the serving size column by 2.5. Too often people will see a label claiming 400 kilojoules of energy, and only 4 grams of fat and assume it is a low-fat, low kilojoule food, only to notice after eating the whole thing, that it is 400 kilojoules per serving with 3 servings in the container. This equals 1200 kilojoules and 12 grams of fat, which is no longer low-fat or low kilojoule.

The label is set up so the servings per container and serving size are on top. These should be the first things read. Then all of the other values can be put into perspective.

INGREDIENTS LIST

The second area of a food label that can be helpful is the ingredient list. It is often below the nutritional information label. As a rule, the ingredients are listed in descending order with the ingredients with the highest quantity listed first. This order allows you to quickly review the main ingredients of a certain product.

At first glance, it may seem like a degree in chemistry is needed to understand most labels, but it's not as hard as it looks. Here are a few important rules to remember when reading the ingredients list:

✓ If you or someone in your family suffers from a food allergy or intolerance, the ingredients list is especially helpful, as it allows you to determine whether or not the product contains the problem food.

✓ The ingredients list also allows consumers to identify and reject products that contain nasty food additives, for example artificial colourings, flavour enhancers, preservatives and antioxidants.

✓ If the first few ingredients are names you cannot pronounce that include numbers, it is most likely a highly processed food with lots of preservatives and colours.

✓ Pay attention to the ingredients in parentheses as these are what make up one of the listed ingredients.

✓ Watch out for words like hydrogenated oils, added sucrose, dextrose, maltose (or any other sugars), artificial colouring or flavouring, and anything listed as a food product instead of a whole food.

✓ Even water may have a list of ingredients in parentheses after it if products have been added to the water.

In addition to the ingredients list, food labels must include a warning of the health risks associated with certain ingredients. For example, products containing peanuts, aspartame, quinine, caffeine, guarana, royal jelly, or un-pasteurized milk or eggs must visibly note the specific ingredient, and warn of the health risk associated with it.

OTHER COMPONENTS OF FOOD PACKAGING

Food packaging also contains other information that can help you make healthy selections for you and your family.

✓ **'Use By' and 'Best Before' Dates**
Expiration dates on packaged food takes one of two forms, both of which mean entirely different things. A 'Best Before' date indicates that a product will retain its taste, quality, and nutritional value up to the stated date, although it will still be safe to consume after that date. However, a 'Use By' date indicates that a product will not be safe to consume after the expiration date has passed.

✓ **Recommended Storage**
The recommended storage method for a product is also stated on the label. This indicates how you should store the product in order to best preserve its taste, quality, and nutritional value. For example, labels may recommend that you refrigerate the product after opening it, or store it in a cool, dry place.

✓ **Organic-Certified Produce**
There is a growing market for food that is labelled as organic-certified produce. Organic farmers and food producers grow and produce food without using synthetic chemicals like pesticides or artificial fertilizers. Issues of animal welfare and environmental sustainability are also important to organic farmers; for example, chickens are free range and not kept in cages, and animals are not fed any growth-regulating drugs, steroids, hormones or antibiotics. Organic standards are enforced by registered organic certification groups. If in doubt, check the packaging and look for a logo belonging to one or another of these authorities.

READING FOOD LABELS FOR A HEALTHIER DIET

The healthiest foods are natural foods. Preservatives, and most additives, in small quantities are not a serious health concern, but should be kept to a minimum where possible. Choosing natural selections when available is a much better choice. When buying packaged foods be sure to read the labels, paying particular attention to the nutritional information panel and the ingredients list.

Remember, food labels are a great way to counter some of the misinformation associated with food marketing and packaging, and it takes only a second to turn a product over and scan the label. This simple action can help eliminate a lot of the hidden sugars, fats and kilojoules in the diet. It can also help avoid many harmful ingredients and additives. Also watch out for serving sizes and servings per container, as many companies lower the recommended serving size to make their product appear to be a healthy choice. Make an effort to teach children to be conscious of what is in foods; they can be taught to read labels also.

QUICK TIPS FOR PARENTS

✓ Know the difference between marketing and informing.

✓ Understand how guidelines affect a food manufacturer's claims.

✓ Consider the hidden meaning of nutrition claims and slogans.

✓ Read the nutritional information panel for a complete understanding of a product's nutritional value.

✓ Use the amount per serving column to calculate daily intakes.

✓ Use the amount per 100g/100ml column to compare different products' nutritional content.

✓ Read the ingredients list to ensure products don't contain ingredients you or someone in your family is allergic to or intolerant of.

✓ Avoid products with additives, particularly those that have been linked to health and behavioural issues in children.

✓ Pay attention to warnings of health risks associated with specific ingredients.

✓ Take note of 'used by' and 'best before' dates, and store food as recommended to avoid spoiling or contamination.

✓ Check food labels for other pertinent information.

8

Life: Be In It

Understanding the importance of exercise and being active

Quick Chapter Guide

- ✔ The importance of exercise for children and adults
- ✔ Age-appropriate activities and activities for families
- ✔ Traditional versus non-traditional activities
- ✔ Integrating activity into everyday life
- ✔ Short-term versus long-term goals
- ✔ Using incentives and rewards
- ✔ Avoiding discouragement
- ✔ Developing a successful fitness plan

Life: Be In It

Understanding the importance of exercise and being active

If you are concerned about your family's health, regular activity is an important part of a healthy living plan. Particularly for children, exercise is critical for the development of strong bodies and the maintenance of good health. If your kids are not getting enough regular activity, the changes you make now to remedy this will have a positive effect on their health well into adulthood and old age. The type of exercise chosen is less important than the choice to exercise. And nowadays, there are almost endless options for increasing physical activity.

THE BENEFITS OF BEING ACTIVE

Being physically active has many benefits for both children and adults. Exercise strengthens the heart and lungs, improving endurance. Exercise also builds strong muscles, bones, ligaments, and tendons, all of which are especially important in growing children. Other physical benefits include improved digestion and an increase in one's energy levels.

Although these benefits are considerable, regular exercise affects more than just physical health. Children and adults who are physically active are generally happier and are able to concentrate better, leading to better performance in school and at work. This is partly because physical activity increases the blood flow to the brain, allowing the brain more oxygen, and partly because of the release of certain hormones during and immediately after exercising. Regular activity also provides a way to release stress, helping to improve mental and emotional wellbeing.

Frequent exercise is also effective as a preventative measure. Physically active children and adults are less likely to develop medical conditions such as diabetes, heart disease, asthma, and even some cancers. Exercise has also been proven to delay the onset of symptoms in some joint and muscle disorders, as well as the effects of aging itself.

In other words, no matter how old you are, regular activity is good for you. It improves your physical, mental, and emotional health, and can delay or even prevent certain medical conditions. A healthier exercise plan is important to every member of your family.

AGE-APPROPRIATE ACTIVITIES

Most adults think of exercise as a trip to the gym - at best, a tedious chore. However, children typically have a different approach, which you can observe at the local park, on a schoolyard, even on your own street. What adults call exercise, kids call play.

Unfortunately, more and more children's pastimes are becoming sedentary, and kids today are spending too much time in front of the television or computer, motionless for hours on end. In order to reverse the trend, you will need to think back to what you liked to do as a child. It is your job to teach your children how to play again.

What you and your children decide to do is not important, so long as it is active. There are countless ways to get

Research shows that physical activity:

- Builds strong bones and strengthens muscles
- Promotes good posture and balance
- Increases relaxation
- Maintains flexibility
- Enhances healthy growth and development
- Strengthens the heart
- Achieves a healthy weight
- Improves fitness
- Improves physical self-esteem
- Helps children to meet new friends

exercise and have fun too; you are limited only by your imagination. However, when planning activities for your children, it is important to keep their ages in mind. Children in different developmental stages have different physical and mental capabilities, and your activities will need to take their requirements into account.

It's also important to understand the different types of exercise and the benefits of combining play based activities or traditional sports that include:

- ✓ Flexibility activities like bending, moving and stretching to help relax the muscles and joints; keeping them mobile and preventing injury.
- ✓ Strength or resistance activities to help build muscles and bones, and improve posture.
- ✓ Endurance or aerobic activities that involve continuous movement like playing catch, power walking and jogging to give your heart, lungs and circulatory system a workout.

A balance between flexibility, strength, and aerobic activities helps promote better overall health and fitness and avoid injury. Consider the importance of a balance between these activity types when planning family exercise and play.

Activities for 0-2 Year Olds

In the first 2 years of life, your child is in a constant state of exploration. In infancy, your child's focus is on learning new skills, such as lifting their head, grasping a toy, rolling over, or sitting up. As a result, your baby needs plenty of encouragement to practise these skills. Simply giving them plenty of time on the floor, with bright, interesting toys nearby to stimulate curiosity, will ensure they get the exercise their body needs.

As your baby grows older, they will begin to acquire skills that enable them to roam at will. Everything is still new, and with each step they encounter something else to investigate. You may notice that your child is into almost everything, just as soon as they are able. Unsurprisingly, the activities appropriate for this age will give your child the opportunity to explore – safely – their body and surroundings. Encouraging toddlers to walk rather than be carried or ride in a stroller will help their legs become strong, even if it slows you down a little.

Activity Suggestions

- ✓ Allow your infant plenty of floor time, with several colourful toys nearby to spark their attention.
- ✓ Encourage your toddler to walk at every opportunity, even if it means you have to slow your pace a little. Simple games are perfect for infants and toddlers, as they encourage movement without requiring too many gross and fine motor skills.
- ✓ Children who can walk enjoy participating in games like "Ring-a-Ring o' Roses".

Activities for 2-5 Year Olds

As with infants and toddlers, most preschool age children need little direction in keeping active. At this age, the television may be a new discovery for your child, but as the parent you still have almost complete control over how much exposure to TV they receive. For the most part, your preschooler is still exploring their body and the skills they acquire almost every day. However, as your preschooler grows stronger and more capable, they also require bigger challenges than they did as an infant or toddler.

In general, preschool children love equipment that allows them to practise their blossoming gross motor skills. Trips to the playground, riding tricycles and bicycles, and other gross motor activities will be popular with your preschooler.

Activity Suggestions

- ✓ Allow your child to continue to explore and practise new skills.
- ✓ Provide your child with a swing set or take them to a playground, where they can practise gross motor skills.
- ✓ Give your child a tricycle or a bicycle with training wheels to help build strong legs.
- ✓ Play simple games with your child, such as chase.
- ✓ Invite other children to join you and your child in group games.

Activities for School Age Children and Families

One of the most enjoyable things about seeing your child grow is being able to relate to them on new levels. Physical activity becomes more fun as kids develop a deeper understanding of concepts such as complicated rules, enabling you to play more engaging games together. Family games become more central to a school age child's activity plan as they become better at interacting with their playmates, allowing for small group games that involve the whole family.

There are a variety of traditional and non-traditional activities to entertain your child. However, it is important to allow them the freedom to explore different activities and participate in the ones they like best. There are also a number of options for working activity into everyday routines. With a little family effort and motivation, school age children and teens can be encouraged to maintain a healthy, active lifestyle.

Traditional Activities

There are plenty of traditional activities for your child to explore. Team sports, athletics, dance and martial arts, strength training and exercise classes can all help kids improve their motor skills and physical health, as well as skills such as thinking quickly, working as part of a team, and planning strategies.

Traditional activities make great family activities, too. A touch football game for the entire family can turn out to be so much fun that everyone forgets they are exercising. Many traditional activities, such as playing catch in the yard, are also easy to play with little equipment.

The downfall to traditional activities is that they often carry with them a high emphasis on competition. As competition is frequently a deterrent to children, care should be taken to play it down as much as possible.

Traditional activities for school age children and families can be as simple as going for family walks. In fact, going for a walk a few times a week is a great way to start a family fitness plan. Other traditional activities such as team sports, dance, martial arts, exercise classes and strength training are available from your child's school or outside organizations. However, it should be noted that strength training should be reserved for teens and adults; during middle childhood, your child will get all the strength-building activity they need through active play.

Activity Suggestions

✓ Enroll your child in a sports team or class of their choosing.

✓ Plan family ball games or other family activities.

✓ Go for walks and/or hikes.

✓ Go on bike rides.

✓ Guide your teen in appropriate strength training methods.

✓ Avoid excessive emphasis on competition.

Non-Traditional Activities

Not all children are well suited to sports and other traditional activities. Many children will be more open to exercising if activities take a less traditional route. Cooperative activities – activities in which everyone participates toward a common goal – might put a child who is sensitive to competition at ease. Individual activities and non-traditional classes may also be good alternatives, for example skateboarding, bike riding, and rollerblading, walking the dog, rock climbing, bowling, yoga, music lessons, drama and dance classes.

Activity Suggestions

✓ Set a family goal, such as a number of kilometres walked or a number of stairs climbed during the day.

✓ Have a family relay race where everyone is on the same team.

✓ Organize a scavenger hunt.

✓ Encourage your child to create their own games.

✓ Look for organized activities that are less traditional, with less emphasis on competition.

INTEGRATING ACTIVITY INTO EVERYDAY LIFE

Scheduled activities or playtime are not the only way to increase your family's activity levels. There are many choices that children and adults alike make during the course of each day that decrease their overall activity levels. Committing to a healthy lifestyle requires taking a closer look at your family's habits, and deciding where different decisions can help to improve your activity levels and quality of life.

Getting From Place to Place

For the children of previous generations, going somewhere meant walking or riding a bike, rather than simply asking a parent for a ride. This difference in lifestyle alone has resulted in a sharp decrease in children's activity levels. Therefore, one way you can encourage your child to be more active is to limit the availability of rides. If the place they desire to go is within walking distance, and the route there is safe, there is simply no reason to give them a ride!

✓ Have your child walk to and from school, or walk with them, rather than driving. If school is too far away, your child can walk to and from the bus stop, or you can make a habit of dropping them off and picking them up a short distance from school.

✓ Get into the habit of walking or riding your bike places, such as work, the shops, restaurants, and even the grocery store, on occasions where you only have a few items to pick up.

✓ Don't drive your child to and from any place that is close enough to walk or ride a bike to.

✓ Take the stairs rather than escalators and lifts.

Getting Exercise Around the House

Even normal household chores can be a source of physical activity. If you haven't already, make up a list of chores for your child to take responsibility for, both indoors and outdoors.

✓ Ask kids to clean their own rooms. Letting them turn their music up while they work can help keep kids moving and involved.

✓ Allow your child to remodel and rearrange their room frequently – with approval and supervision, of course. Painting, moving furniture, and building shelves or cabinets are terrific ways of staying active, not to mention learning new skills.

✓ Assign your child chores such as vacuuming and sweeping.

✓ Encourage your child to help with yard work. Requesting your child's aid in raking grass and leaves, trimming shrubs, and tending the garden is an effective way to encourage a sedentary child outside. Letting young children jump in the leaves, experiment with shaping shrubs, or make decisions on the contents and layout of the garden can all act as extra incentive.

Sprucing Up Sedentary Pastimes

Adults and children alike tend to spend down time in sedentary pastimes, like watching TV, reading, or talking on the phone. Office work, school and supermarket queues also require people to stand still for long periods of time. All of these activities steal time that could otherwise be spent exercising. However, the habits of a more active lifestyle can also be applied to these pastimes, increasing the overall exercise you and your family get throughout the day.

✓ When watching TV, stretch and/or move around during commercials. Jogging in place, doing jumping jacks, walking back and forth, even just getting up for a few minutes wakes the body up.

✓ Get into the habit of pacing while you talk on the phone. Requiring that your teens to do the same ensures that the time they spend on the phone contributes to their overall activity level, rather than subtracting from it.

✓ Any other time you find yourself sitting or standing still, make a conscious effort to stretch and move around from time to time.

Activities for a Rainy Day

For people who enjoy exercising outdoors, poor weather can be a disappointment. However, you don't have to let a little rain scare you away from achieving a more active lifestyle! Even if you don't want to venture outside, there are plenty of other ways to get your child – and yourself – moving.

✓ Dress in a good rain suit and head outside anyway. Most kids love to play in the rain, so you shouldn't hear many complaints. Just act like they're getting to do something that is normally unheard of, and they'll be so excited about breaking the rules that your biggest problem will be getting them inside again later.

✓ If possible, set aside an area of the house devoted to indoor gross motor play.

✓ Pull the cars out of the garage and let your child ride their bike inside or play games like handball and basketball.

✓ Find an active game to play, such as charades.

✓ Put an exercise video in the DVD player and clear the floor. Whether or not everyone takes it seriously, the important thing is that you're active!

✓ Children love to dance! Put on some good music and let them take it away!

SETTING GOALS AND MAINTAINING DIRECTION

The goals you set are one of the most important parts of your family's fitness plan, as they serve to keep you on track. The first step is to decide why the family is committing to a healthier, more active lifestyle. Whether it is to improve everyone's general physical health, or to lose or manage weight, coming to an agreement between the entire family is an important part of starting a new fitness plan.

Once your family has identified the reasons for pursuing your new lifestyle, you will be able to set group goals accordingly. Having this direction not only affects the types of activities you and your family choose to make a part of your fitness plan, it also helps keep the family focused.

Remember all activity plans should have a balance between flexibility, resistance and aerobic conditioning. For weight maintenance or to improve cardiovascular health a program with a strong aerobic component and a small amount of flexibility and resistance activity is appropriate. For general fitness, weight loss, or those suffering from joint pain or other orthopedic concerns regular activities with equal parts flexibility, resistance and aerobic conditioning are recommended.

> **"For the average teenager, a brisk 30 minute walk burns about 500 kilojoules, jogging for the same duration close to 1000kJ, and running about 1500kJ. To burn 37000kJ or a kilo of fat, the teen would need to do 35 hours of walking, 17 ½ hours of jogging, or 12 hours of running."**

Short-Term vs Long-Term Goals

Setting short-term, attainable goals, is important to keep everyone focused. If the only goal is a long-term goal that may take a year or more to reach, family members will become discouraged fairly quickly. Short-term goals offer more immediate feedback on the progress of your new activity plan. Additionally, as each short-term goal is reached a feeling of accomplishment accompanies it. This leads to a boost in motivation and a rededication to continuing activity and goal setting. The key to success is short-term goals that lead to mid- and longer-term goals.

Appropriate short-term goals should present family members with achievements that are easily obtained, yet bring everyone a step closer to reaching their ultimate goal. Goals should start out small, gradually becoming more challenging as they are achieved.

Appropriate short-term goals might include:

- ✓ Adding 20-30 minutes of exercise 3-4 times a week to start.
- ✓ Decreasing daily television viewing to one or two favourite shows.
- ✓ Finding a weekly sports team or exercise class to participate in.
- ✓ Making time for just one family activity per week.

- ✓ Being more active while on the phone or during television breaks.
- ✓ Walking to places more often, and making the choice to take the stairs rather than lifts and escalators.
- ✓ Sharing family chores and tasks around the home that promote activity.

Again, the biggest advantage of using short-term goals in your family fitness plan is that the achievement of small goals naturally creates a system of incentives and rewards. Knowing that they have accomplished something they set out to do rewards and motivates kids by making them feel good about their efforts, and gives them confidence to continue towards the next set of goals.

Using Incentives and Rewards

Although the achievement of goals can create natural incentives, parents must be wary of using artificial rewards to encourage their children. If not used properly, rewards can backfire by implying that exercise is a chore, rather than an activity to be enjoyed.

Sometimes, however, children will need a few rewards to get started, before they discover that being physically active has its own rewards. In these cases, the reward system should taper off as your child discovers the natural rewards of physical activity, such as the achievement of smaller goals, weight loss, and improved self-esteem. Artificial rewards should also be related to the goal in some way. Some examples of appropriate rewards include:

- ✓ An earned amount of TV or game time, such as 30 seconds for every minute spent exercising.
- ✓ Rewards geared toward the whole family, such as a night out to celebrate reaching a family goal.
- ✓ New clothes as your child loses weight.
- ✓ Charts to track each family member's progress.
- ✓ Praise and acknowledgement of a job well done.

Although it might be tempting to use special treats as a reward, this sends your child the wrong message by reinforcing poor nutritional choices. Instead, consider using your child's cravings to teach a valuable message. Calculate the amount of activity required to burn the kilojoules in your child's favourite treat, and explain that in order to eat the treat, they will have to exercise appropriately to counteract the excess kilojoules.

Avoiding Discouragement

Just as some things can help motivate children, other things can discourage them and make them want to quit. In order to prevent your child from giving up and returning to their pre-activity habits, it is important to avoid pitfalls like:

- ✓ Focusing too much on competition.
- ✓ Making goals too tough to attain.
- ✓ Starting a fitness program too quickly, without a gradual adjustment period.
- ✓ Criticizing your child.

DEVELOPING A SUCCESSFUL FITNESS PLAN

The fitness plan you and your family develop together is important, since it will have a bearing on whether you succeed. If your fitness plan is carefully created, it will help your family make the transition to becoming more physically active. Because physical activity is such a vital part of your family's health, it is important to carefully consider how you plan to bring about this important change.

One of the most significant factors in a successful fitness plan is how much fun you make it. Forcing kids to do something they don't enjoy will only create resistance and rebellion. However, if you let children choose the activities that most interest them, schedule fun family activities, and frequently include your child's friends, chances are kids will forget that they are exercising and simply have fun. The same goes for adults: a boring fitness routine is difficult to stick with, but you will find that scheduling family activities and playing with your kids makes staying fit easy and fun.

When planning a family exercise plan keep it simple and make it fun. Remember: small attainable goals and lots of encouragement are most important.

QUICK TIPS FOR PARENTS

Families with young children (10 and younger):

- ✓ Choose activities that are age appropriate.
- ✓ Avoid resistance exercises, except those involved in normal play.
- ✓ Join in with them - kids love to have their parents play along.
- ✓ Let kids experiment with a lot of activities and exercises so they will develop a well rounded program and can find their own strengths.
- ✓ Sport activities should be done for fun.
- ✓ Simple competition is fine but should not be stressed.
- ✓ Encourage school aged children to join organized sports teams or classes such as dance, gymnastics or other individual sports.
- ✓ Avoid forcing children into activities that they dislike.
- ✓ Play! It is the best form of exercise for any age, but especially for younger children.

Families with older children and teens:

- ✓ Let older kids and teens guide the activities with a little input from parents - they tend to get involved more if it is their idea.
- ✓ Let the competition become a little more focused.
- ✓ Don't hesitate to try new activities. If kids suggest it give it a try.
- ✓ 4-5 days a week of exercise activities for older children is recommended because they tend to get less activity in school and on their own.
- ✓ Encourage them to try different sports. They may find they are good at sports they had no idea about.
- ✓ Encourage them to get friends involved as well. They may be more willing to do activities with their friends.
- ✓ If they were involved in organized sports or other activities when they were younger encourage them to stay involved (or get involved again).
- ✓ Look for lifetime fitness activities that will help them develop healthy habits for life. Skiing, golf (without a cart), biking, hiking, canoeing/kayaking, and swimming are all great lifetime fitness activities.
- ✓ Keep it fun.

For free downloadable activity planners and other useful information to help you get started visit
www.abcfitkids.com/activityisfun

9

Parents as Role Models

Encouraging better family health and wellbeing begins at home

Quick Chapter Guide

- ✔ Creating commitment: parents as role models
- ✔ Being active together: planning family activities isn't as hard as you think
- ✔ The importance of individual exercise
- ✔ Motivating kids and parents
- ✔ Making time for healthy meals together
- ✔ The importance of quality family time to connect
- ✔ Teaching independent decision making skills and fostering good individual habits
- ✔ Keeping track of progress and celebrating success

Parents as Role Models

Encouraging better family health and wellbeing begins at home

Children are influenced by friends, the media, sports stars, and influential adults. But the most influential people, especially for younger children, are their parents. At times it may appear that any of the other influences has more impact but parents have the first, last, and most important influence on children.

Creating Commitment: Parents as Role Models

As kids grow, so do the influences they are susceptible to outside the home. Therefore, the earlier you establish healthy habits in your child, the better. Studies have shown that family time seems to be the one consistent factor in overall health in children. Kids who have involved parents perform better in school, have better emotional health, have higher self-esteem and are more willing to try new experiences.

Parents' influence on children may come from direct involvement, for example, by teaching kids about healthy choices, setting up exercise routines, signing them up for classes or sports activities, and telling them what to eat. Even more effective, though, are the indirect influences that are a result of leading by example.

Too often parents will lead by the "Do as I say, not as I do" motto. This sends mixed messages. It also leads to children believing that the healthy lifestyle is only important when their parents are watching. Modelling the desired behaviour and leading by example will help children take up healthier habits in the long run.

Living a healthy lifestyle and modelling good exercise habits will show children how important these factors are. They will see their parents eating the same foods they do. They will be exercising just like mum and dad do. The joy of exercising and eating healthy foods will be secondary to the feeling of family togetherness. Younger children especially like to imitate their parents and are eager to please. Parents are their first heroes. They consider something okay if they see mum and dad doing it. They will try harder and go longer when keeping up with their parents.

Developing the habit early on is important. As children get older it is harder to get them to try new family activities. They generally have a set schedule that is to their liking and don't want to have to change it. Although parental influence is still there, and many kids want some direction and control from their parents, peer and social pressure often make it difficult to reach these children. Teens, and even pre-teens, will often throw out the "But you don't (or do) do it" excuse if they are asked to commit to different activities or eat different foods and beverages. Consequently, modelling and leading by example becomes even more important at this stage.

Often leading by example encourages children to be more active. If parents are going out for a hike younger children have to go. Most children find it easier, and more fun, to just join in than to try to find ways out of it. Parental habits and lifestyle play a big role in children's developing habits. Healthy, active parents tend to raise healthy, active children.

Being Active Together

An increase in family time allows for communication, activity and learning. Families who communicate have a better understanding of each other and develop closeness. This helps foster emotional health as well.

Family activities take a little more planning and scheduling but they are great for overall health. Getting everyone together can be tough on a busy family. Most families have common times when they are all together, for example during meal times, after work and school, and before bed. Use these times to plan short activities that will enhance everyone's fitness levels. Weekends are a great time to plan bigger events. A family hike and picnic with healthy meal choices is a great way to get everyone together and active. A family game of Frisbee after the picnic will increase overall activity levels. Plan family activities just like doctor or dentist appointments. Write them on the calendar and stick to them. This will reinforce the importance of these times.

Family activities do not need to be planned down to the last detail. Just pick the time and place, if appropriate have some sports equipment available, and see what happens. Playing handball, shooting hoops, walking and bike riding, playing tag or hide and seek, having water balloon or squirt gun wars, and swimming at the beach are great family activities that can be enjoyed by everyone and that don't require a lot of planning.

The lesson here is that the activity chosen is not important. Simply get the family together and let the fun develop.

Individual Exercise

Although family together time is important it is sometimes difficult to come by when a busy schedule encroaches. Allowing individual exercise options is important as well.

Encourage children to participate in individual activities and model this by doing the same. A gym membership and consistent exercise routine will demonstrate the importance of exercise for a healthy lifestyle. Stick to it and encourage the children to do the same. Not every activity can be a family activity and that is okay. The key is to increase exercise participation through any means possible.

MOTIVATION

We all need to be motivated at times to follow through with healthy choices. It can be difficult when there are other demands on time and energy - being the ambassador of change can be exhausting, especially when you are trying to orchestrate a significant turnaround in your family's lifestyle. From time to time, you are bound to lose your motivation. It is at times like this when small steps and your decision to involve the entire family will pay off, with everyone working together to stay on track.

Motivating Kids

Motivation for kids to eat healthily and get more exercise, especially for young kids, needs to be external at first. Kids won't choose to eat healthy meals on their own. Additionally, most children, when asked, will say they get enough exercise on their own.

Parents need to be creative to motivate kids and teens to eat well and exercise. At the same time it is important to stress the importance of healthy meals and increased activity so children can learn to motivate themselves.

Using rewards and incentives can help motivate kids to get moving. However these motivators can create their own problems and can sometimes lead to exercising and eating right for the wrong reasons. If a child only completes an exercise routine or eats the vegetables on the plate to get a reward, when rewards are withdrawn the motivation to exercise and eat right might be as well. If rewards are going to be used as motivators, use them randomly and taper them off over time, and as your child makes progress.

Living a healthy life and letting the kids see the benefits is a great motivator as well. Seeing mum or dad bound up the stairs, or join them romping outside, is a great way for kids to see the value of healthy living. Children, especially older kids, will definitely be motivated to exercise more and eat better if they have a hard time keeping up with their parents.

Making an activity a fun, family event will also help to motivate children to join in. Drab exercise routines that require multiple repetitions of exercises may turn kids off exercise. But dynamic activities that change often and involve a little excitement will help bring the kids on board. Inviting children's friends to join in can also help to motivate them. If they know they can spend more time with their friends they will be willing to do more.

Motivating kids to eat healthily and exercise can be as easy as leading by example. Motivation will eventually come from within when they see the results and experience the positive effects, but until then lead a healthy lifestyle and bring the kids on board in any way possible.

Motivating Each Other

Sometimes the kids are not the only ones who need motivating. With household responsibilities, work and study, time can become a factor working against the program. It's important for parents to work together to motivate each other and share responsibility. When you feel tired or discouraged, one way to restore your motivation is to take a break and indulge in some leisure time you really enjoy. This can be done together as a family, for example by taking a trip to the movies or a favourite restaurant, or you may choose something that is personally gratifying and take individual time outs.

Keeping records of the progress you and your family make, such as tracking accomplishments or putting family activities in writing, also helps maintain motivation. And of course, the more fun you are having, the less you will struggle with motivational issues.

A few key points to remember when the motivation starts to lag:

- ✓ Remind each other that it is for the kids' health as well as your own.
- ✓ Post a motivating message on the bathroom mirror.
- ✓ Pull out the 'before' photos to remind you of why the program was started.
- ✓ Pick a favourite activity and get out and play it together for fun.
- ✓ Write the dates and times of family activities in the daily planner just as you would for any other important meeting.
- ✓ If your spouse always does the cooking, offer to take over for a night.
- ✓ Keep it fun!

Motivating the kids is important but don't forget motivation is needed for everyone from time to time. Even the most dedicated athletes have moments when their motivation slides. Lifestyle changes can be difficult for everyone but if you take it slow, and keep it fun and simple, it will happen.

HEALTHY MEALS TOGETHER

Meal times used to be a big family event, especially the evening meal. When the work and school day was done and all chores were completed the family all sat down to a nice home-cooked meal. Those days are gone and now it is often a meal on the fly between meetings, practices and other commitments. Families need to take back some of that time and sit down to some healthy home-cooked meals again. Family meals may be breakfast during the week, lunch on the weekends, or dinner a few nights a week – it doesn't matter when. What is important is that you and your family have an opportunity to touch base, and that you as a parent have an opportunity to model and encourage healthy eating habits.

Sitting down to a family meal allows for control of what is eaten and opens up lines of communication not available during meals on the run. When everyone is sitting around the table and the aroma of fresh cooked foods wakes up the taste buds the family time is special. Current events, the latest gossip, or future plans are all topics for discussion at this time. Parents who take the time to listen can learn a lot from these meal times.

This is also a valuable time of rest and re-energizing. It is a time when children can talk with their parents without

competing with office pressures or the ringing of the telephone. Parents have their children's attention and can talk about important moral or social issues while keeping it light and enjoyable. Both sides can enjoy the give and take of relaxed conversation over good food. Table manners and etiquette can be modelled and taught at this time as well.

When parents eat healthy choices in proper proportions during the meal, it will help children develop their own healthy habits. Parents who model this behaviour will find children following suit eventually.

Make time for healthy meal preparation by having ingredients ready ahead of time and then enlist everyone's help to set and clear the table. Grocery shopping, meal planning, food preparation, and even dishwashing can be an opportunity to involve everyone. Most children and teens enjoy helping in the kitchen, and with the proper encouragement they will enjoy putting together their own meals as well. Getting everyone's assistance in washing the dishes and cleaning up is also a great way to conclude a meal. Working together makes family meals more enjoyable and a realistic possibility for everyone.

At times when everyone is too busy to share a family meal, making sure that your kitchen and pantry are well stocked with healthy, delicious food choices will ensure your kids are able to make snacks and late dinners on their own - without spoiling the plan with junk and convenience foods.

QUICK TIPS FOR PARENTS

- ✓ Be creative to motivate kids and teens to eat right and exercise.
- ✓ Maintain a commitment to supporting each other.
- ✓ Schedule family activities to make exercising more fun and foster good relationships.
- ✓ Avoid trying to plan the entire activity.
- ✓ Plan family meals as frequently as everyone's schedules will allow.
- ✓ Get family members involved in food preparation before the meal, and the clean-up afterward.
- ✓ Plan shopping lists together, and keep the pantry stocked with healthy food choices.
- ✓ Remember to take leisure breaks and rewards together and individually.
- ✓ Keep track of the progress you and your family make and celebrate success.
- ✓ Remember the importance of quality family time to connect.
- ✓ Make it fun!

"It is important to remember that as the parent, you are your child's best chance for change. Therefore, the single most powerful impression you can make on your child is to establish an environment where they regularly see, and are expected to imitate, healthy behaviours."

Fostering Good Individual Habits

As important as family meals and activities are to the success of your family's new, healthier lifestyle, it is a fact of life that the entire family can't always be together. If your lifestyle plan is going to be successful, each family member will need to be able to stick to it, even when they are outside the home.

Naturally, if you expect your children to make healthy decisions when you are not present, you will need to model the desired values in your own decisions. Eating healthy lunches at work and finding time to exercise during your own day are great ways to practise these values in your own life. Your child will also eat lunch and play during recess and have the opportunity to participate in physical education classes at school. Take advantage of these moments away from home by encouraging healthy choices and active play.

Although not everything can – or should – be a family activity, that doesn't mean you can't be involved. Taking the time to discuss your day and the choices you made is a good opportunity to reinforce the notion that everyone is encouraged to continue the program away from home. It also allows for parents to give advice and praise.

BEING YOUR CHILD'S BEST CHANCE

Parenting can often be a frustrating endeavour, and the thought of completely changing your family's lifestyle may seem impossible to you. However, it is important to remember that as the parent, you are your child's best chance for change. Therefore, the single most powerful impression you can make on your child is to establish an environment where they regularly see, and are expected to imitate, healthy behaviours.

QUICK TIPS FOR PARENTS

- ✓ Always model the behaviours you want your child to learn.
- ✓ Establish rules, expectations, and a supportive family environment.
- ✓ Use modelling and encouragement rather than coercion.
- ✓ Be there to encourage each other when motivation wanes.
- ✓ Involve the entire family in meals and activities as frequently as possible.
- ✓ Teach independent decision-making skills.
- ✓ Remember the importance of small steps, open discussion with older children and planning.

10

Slow and Steady Wins the Race

Be consistent, take time to rest, and work together

Quick Chapter Guide

- ✔ Understanding the relationship between the body and mind
- ✔ Balancing the physical, psychological and emotional aspects of health
- ✔ Communication skills to build emotional health and trust
- ✔ The benefits of rest and play in relieving stress
- ✔ Allowing for sufficient sleep
- ✔ The importance of regular down time to reenergize
- ✔ Small steps are the key - how a simple plan leads to lasting changes

Slow and Steady Wins the Race

Be consistent, take time to rest, and work together

Although changing your family's lifestyle is a life-defining event, it is not an impossible goal to achieve. Even so, you should not expect to achieve a healthy lifestyle overnight. Individuals and families who fail at their programs often do so because they try to accomplish too much too quickly, without paying enough attention to the needs of the body and mind. Subsequently, when planning your program, it is important to understand the reciprocal relationship between the body and the mind, and the importance of rest.

Health has many factors including physical, psychological and emotional. All of the factors are important for overall health. On one hand, a healthy body leads to a healthy mind; however, ignoring your child's psychological and emotional needs can quickly sabotage your plans and lead to other issues. Healthy habits, such as proper nutrition and regular exercise, affect more than just you and your family's bodies.

A healthy lifestyle has a range of benefits, including:

- ✓ Improving physical health, which helps prevent disease and keeps everyone feeling well.
- ✓ Improving psychological health, which increases motivation and mental stability.
- ✓ Improving emotional health, which encourages self-esteem and a strong feeling of self-worth.

Just as a healthy lifestyle can have a positive effect on mental and emotional aspects of a child's health, neglecting a child's mental and emotional wellbeing can cause problems with their physical health, as many physical disorders are connected with stress. In order to complete your healthy living program, you need to be sure that you address all areas. Proper nutrition and exercise is only part of the picture, and must be combined with solid family communication and encouragement, sufficient amounts of play and rest, and a simple overall approach.

COMMUNICATE AND ENCOURAGE

Communication is the foundation of family relations, and therefore a necessary part of your healthy living program. By communicating with each other, family members are able to share information, express their support for one another, develop plans for the future, and even release stress. It is for this reason that the involvement of the entire family is recommended to make the switch to a healthy lifestyle. Work family time into your schedule, no matter how busy everyone is – and remember to use the chance to talk to one another during these times, whether you are eating, exercising, or sharing quiet time.

When communicating with your child, remember that communication is an exchange. This means each of you needs to be capable of listening when the need arises. Although as a parent, the temptation is often to do most of the talking, listening to your child is just as important. Sometimes this means letting kids guide the conversation. As you listen, you may find that you discover new things, such as issues children and teens need to discuss or interests that might be used as motivation as kids adapt to a healthier lifestyle.

Most of all, however, your family's emotional health depends on being able to communicate well with each other. As you converse with your child, alternating between talking and listening makes them feel important and the focus of your attention, and as a result the trust between you will continually be strengthened. Talking with each other also allows you to constantly learn more about each other, and it allows you to provide emotional support when necessary.

GET OUT THERE AND PLAY!

Play is one of the most important parts of a healthy lifestyle, and not just as a source of exercise. Although play is undoubtedly the best way for your child to get the proper amount of activity each day, it also promotes happiness and helps kids to feel better about themselves. At the same time, play encourages children of all ages to develop natural creativity, as well as teaching them how to take turns and make sure everyone is included – skills that are necessary in the adult world.

The benefits of play are not just for your child. Children and adults alike gain significant advantages from play. For instance, play has been shown to be more beneficial in adults than traditional exercise, improving cardiovascular, respiratory, and mental health more than even the most dedicated gym routine. Additionally, play helps adults maintain their youth for longer, both physically and mentally - adults who play with their children recover and maintain the skills that they haven't used since childhood; they also reduce their stress and improve their own wellbeing.

With all of the benefits to be had from playing with your children, there is absolutely no reason to stay inside while you send them out to play. Enjoy the advantages of having fun, experiencing more motivation, and improving your physical and emotional health all at the same time – get out there and play!

It is also important that everyone gets sufficient time for sleep. It's recommended that young children take regular naps and that older children and adults get an average of 8-9 hours of sleep a night.

A SIMPLE PLAN LEADS TO LASTING CHANGES

Families are often intimidated by the thought of changing their lifestyle because they think it will mean totally uprooting them from everything they are comfortable with. However, a healthier lifestyle simply requires a series of small, bite-size changes. If you try to change everything too quickly, you will only spur resistance in your children and discouragement in yourself – not to mention that you will make it a great deal harder for everyone to achieve their goals. Moreover, your bodies may not be in a position to make drastic changes all at once: overexerting yourself can cause more harm than good, and a strict diet suddenly adopted virtually begs to be broken. You and your family will be much more likely to succeed if you implement small changes a few at a time, mastering each before moving on to the next.

Simple steps means exactly what it sounds like - none of these changes need to be ground-shaking, especially not at first. An acceptable change can simply mean adding family activities or meals a few times a week, gradually reducing the amount of time spent watching television or playing video games, or cutting unhealthy foods out of your family's diet one at a time. Despite the simplicity of these changes, they will be effective if you take the time to master each one - as the changes build, so do the benefits. Once you have turned the corner towards a healthier lifestyle, and the rewards that come from this transition, you will never look back.

REST FOR BETTER HEALTH

Down time is an important part of every individual's day, yet it is often overlooked in busy schedules, until the stress of rushing around all the time begins to wear everyone down. Moreover, even though you may intend to change your lifestyle – slowing down enough to schedule family time and make sure proper nutrition and exercise is not overlooked – you may be ignoring the important role rest plays in your life.

Although you may not feel like you are actually accomplishing anything during quiet time, your body is in fact accomplishing quite a bit. While you rest, your body is able to rebuild and reenergize itself. Muscles and organs are repaired, hormones and metabolism are regulated; even the brain takes the opportunity to revitalize itself.

Despite the importance of taking time to rest and relax throughout the day, don't feel like you have to sit still and do nothing. Down time is a perfect time for family communications or quiet activities. Talk about everyone's day; play a board game; even watch a favourite television program or a family movie. Just remember that resting is as vital to your healthy lifestyle as exercising or eating right.

CHANGING YOUR FAMILY FOR LIFE

Although putting together a well thought out healthy living program may seem overwhelming, it all boils down to one thing: doing what is right for your family.

Remember, it's the small, simple changes that will lead to more permanent results. Trying to make large, wholesale changes will result in resistance and lead to difficulty staying with the changes. Simple does not mean less effective. Small steps accumulated over time will lead to a large change in lifestyle, more permanent weight loss and better health. All together this adds up to a healthier happier family, and teaches children healthy values that will benefit them for the rest of their life.

QUICK TIPS FOR PARENTS

- ✔ Keep your program simple so it's easy to follow.
- ✔ Take small steps toward your ultimate goal.
- ✔ Involve the entire family.
- ✔ Remember to include all aspects of health in your program.
- ✔ Mental and emotional health can be as important as physical health for the development and maintenance of wellbeing.
- ✔ Exercise should be designed to be fun and family oriented.
- ✔ Healthy nutrition should include natural, low-fat, low sugar foods and home cooked, family meals as often as possible.
- ✔ Remember the importance of play – it's the best form of exercise for people of all ages and a great way to improve mental and emotional health.
- ✔ Down time and rest are very important aspects of total health and allow the body to rebuild and reenergize.
- ✔ Allow for sufficient sleep and encourage small children to take frequent naps.
- ✔ Most importantly, keep it simple, take small steps, and develop a program that everyone can live with. Remember this is a lifestyle change not a fad diet or quick fix.

A healthy plan now will result in a healthier future for everyone. Make it an adventure!

For more information visit www.abcfitkids.com

11

It's a Wrap!

Healthy recipes and cooking tips
for the whole family

Quick Chapter Guide

- ✔ Breakfast made easy
- ✔ 5 minute and time-to-spare breakfast ideas
- ✔ The lunch box survival guide
- ✔ Healthy sandwich ideas and nutritious lunch box fillers
- ✔ Speedy dinner delights
- ✔ Nutritious dinner recipes for the whole family
- ✔ Marvelous munchies, snacks and desserts
- ✔ Putting it all together – a week's food planning

It's a Wrap!

Healthy recipes and cooking tips for the whole family

BREAKFAST MADE EASY

Breakfast is an essential meal for everyone in the family, and especially kids. A healthy breakfast restores blood sugar levels after the overnight fast, and provides fuel for the morning. Unfortunately, breakfast is also a time when parents are often at their busiest - packing children off to school and themselves off to work. However a healthy breakfast is not an impossible task, even for the busiest households. All it takes is a little preparation and planning, and a well stocked pantry.

So what are the healthy breakfast choices? Here are some healthy breakfast ideas that can be enjoyed by the whole family. Importantly, always include some whole or sliced fruit with breakfast, and a healthy beverage like a glass of water, low-fat milk, calcium-enriched soy milk, vegetable juice or diluted fruit juice.

5 minute breakfast ideas

✓ Yoghurt and sliced fruit with wholegrain or multigrain toast.

✓ Toasted fruit bagel or english muffin with cream cheese and an apple.

✓ Unsweetened muesli or low-sugar instant cereal like weetbix or corn flakes with low-fat milk or calcium-enriched soy milk, topped with grated apple or diced strawberries.

✓ Rice cakes spread with peanut butter and jam plus an apple.

✓ Berry banana breakfast smoothie made from blended low-fat yoghurt or soy yoghurt, fresh banana, strawberries, ½ cup of water and ¼ cup of wholegrain cereal. Serve with a slice of multigrain toast.

✓ Low-fat savoury or fruit muffin, warmed in the microwave, and served with fruit.

✓ Microwaved porridge with fresh or dried fruit, and low-fat milk or soy milk.

✓ Healthy breakfast bars (opposite) are great for kids on the run. Pack with a small tub of yoghurt, piece of fruit and a 35% juice popper, or small container of milk.

Time-to-spare breakfast ideas

✓ Hard-boiled, poached or scrambled eggs with wholemeal toast soldiers, and some fresh fruit.

✓ Grilled sandwich fingers with ham, tomato and grated low-fat cheese on wholemeal or multigrain bread.

✓ French toast served with a slice of honeydew melon and a dollop of yoghurt.

✓ Breakfast burrito filled with scrambled eggs, baked beans, chopped tomatoes, a little grated cheese, diced ham or other favourite ingredients.

✓ A bowl of old-fashioned porridge made with milk or soy milk. Sweeten with sliced or mashed banana, stewed apple, diced strawberries or a handful of raisins.

✓ Omelette with diced mushroom, corn, baby spinach and low-fat grated cheese. Serve with rye crackers and a slice of watermelon.

✓ Low-fat pancakes with fresh fruit and a light drizzling of honey or a little brown sugar.

✓ Home-made baked bean mix with wholegrain or multigrain toast thinly spread with low-fat cream cheese.

RECIPES

Low-Fat Fruit and Savoury Muffins

PREPARATION TIME

30 minutes

Makes 10-12 muffins

STORAGE

Allow to cool before
serving. Refrigerate in
an airtight container
for up to 5 days.
Great to freeze!

2 cups wholemeal flour
¾ cup processed bran cereal
¾ cup rolled oats
½ cup sugar
3 tsp. baking powder

1 cup low-fat fruit yoghurt
1 cup low-fat milk
1 egg
1 cup berries or 2 mashed bananas

*For savoury muffins use plain low-fat yoghurt
and 1 cup of mixed grated low-fat cheese, diced
mushrooms and spinach or ham.
Combine flour, cereal, oats, sugar and baking
powder. Mix in yoghurt, milk and egg.
Add cup of fruit or savoury mix.
Fill muffin tray 2/3 full.
Bake for 20 minutes at 200°C.
Allow to cool, serve with fruit and a glass of
low-fat milk or soy milk.

Healthy Breakfast Bars

PREPARATION TIME

40 minutes

Makes 12 bars

STORAGE

Refrigerate in
an airtight container
for up to 5 days.
Great to freeze!

1 cup mashed banana
1 cup chopped dried apricots or
   dried mixed fruit medley
1 cup chopped dates
½ cup flaked coconut

1 ¼ cup toasted rolled oats
½ cup wheat germ
½ cup sunflower seeds
¾ cup orange juice
2 tbsp. olive oil and 3 tbsp. runny honey

Preheat oven to 200°C.
Place all ingredients in a bowl and mix until thoroughly combined.
Press mixture into a lightly oiled and lined baking tray.
Mark into bars with a knife.
Bake for 30 minutes until brown.
Allow to cool. Serve with fresh fruit and a glass of low-fat milk or soy milk.

Microwave Porridge with Dried Fruit

PREPARATION TIME

5 minutes

Makes 1-2 servings for
kids or 1 for adults

STORAGE

Best served
immediately.

½ cup rolled oats
handful of dried apricots or apple

½ cup low-fat milk or soy milk
½ cup water

Place the oats and dried fruit into a microwave
safe bowl.
Add the milk and water, mixing well.
Microwave on high for 3-4 minutes.
Serve with extra milk or yoghurt, fresh berries
and a glass of diluted fruit juice.

French Toast

PREPARATION TIME

10 minutes

Makes 1-2 servings for kids or 1 for adults

STORAGE

Best served immediately.

1 egg
1 tbsp. milk
2-3 drops vanilla extract

2 slices wholemeal or multigrain bread, cut into triangles or fingers
1 tbsp. olive oil
honey and fresh berries

Mix the egg, milk, and vanilla extract in a flat bowl.
Soak bread in the mixture so that it is coated evenly on both sides.
Heat oil in pan over medium heat.
Add bread shapes and fry until golden brown on both sides.
Drizzle lightly with honey and serve with some fruit.

Home-Made Baked Beans

PREPARATION TIME

20-25 minutes

Makes 4 servings for kids or 2-3 servings for adults

STORAGE

Can be made the night before and refrigerated for breakfast.

1 small onion, chopped
4 medium tomatoes, chopped
1 tbsp. tomato paste
½ small apple, chopped
⅔ cup water

1 tsp. mixed herbs
½ tsp. mustard powder
1 large tin three bean mix, rinsed
1 tsp. brown sugar

Fry the onion in a splash of olive oil until soft.
Add the tomatoes, tomato paste, apple and water and reduce down by boiling for 5 minutes.
Add the herbs and mustard powder, mix well and leave to cool for a few minutes.
Blend mixture quickly and then return to the pan with the beans. Cook on a low heat for 5-10 minutes.
Add the sugar, stir well and serve.
Serve with wholemeal or multigrain toast thinly spread with low-fat cream cheese.

Banana and Coconut Pancakes

PREPARATION TIME

10 minutes

Makes 8-10 pancakes

STORAGE

Best served immediately. Mixture can be made the night before and refrigerated for breakfast.

1 egg
1¼ cups self-raising flour

1 cup low-fat milk
1 tbsp. olive oil
¼ cup chopped banana
2 tbsp. coconut shavings

Mix the egg, flour, milk and oil in a bowl until smooth.
Stir in the banana and coconut.
Heat a large frying pan and coat lightly with olive oil.
Drop 3-4 spoonfuls of mixture in even spots, tilting the pan to spread the pancakes.
Cook on medium heat until bubbles appear and the bottom is golden brown, then flip and cook other side until golden.
Serve immediately or keep warm in oven until all are cooked. Serve with sliced banana or strawberry and a drizzle of honey to taste.

LUNCH BOX SURVIVAL GUIDE

Packing the school lunch box may seem daunting; however it's not as hard as it sounds. Involving kids in lunch box choices and focusing on food variety helps to make lunch boxes more interesting and provides food balance for the energy kids need to sustain study and play activities throughout the day.

Preparation and planning is the key to stress-free lunch boxes. Make a list of healthy lunch foods and lunch box fillers, and stock your kitchen accordingly. Share the list with your children and ask them to choose which foods they'd like to take to school. Encourage older children and teens to pack their own school lunches, making sure you have plenty of choices on hand for them to choose from each day.

Here are the basics to packing a healthy balanced lunch box that kids will enjoy:

- ✓ Pack a variety of food in small portions and include sufficient snacks to sustain kids through morning tea and lunch periods.
- ✓ Add variety to sandwiches and rolls by using different breads such as wholemeal, multigrain, and rye; english muffins; pitta pockets; tortilla wraps; bagels and fruit bread.
- ✓ As a break from sandwiches try rice, noodle or pasta salads; healthy pizza slices; quiche and frittatas; sushi rolls, and mixed salads with tuna, chicken, or tofu, served with a fresh roll.
- ✓ Home-made soups and stews in a wide-mouthed thermos are also great to break up winter lunch routines and provide a nourishing alternative.
- ✓ For sandwich fillings use protein rich ingredients with salad or vegetables, for example lean meat, chicken, turkey, tuna, egg, peanut butter, kidney beans, hummus or various types of fat reduced cheese.
- ✓ Always include a portion of fresh or canned fruit or vegetables in the lunch box, such as cherry tomatoes; carrot or celery sticks with peanut butter or hummus dip; strawberries; a piece of fruit; fruit salad; dried fruit mix or a small tub of fruit in natural juice.
- ✓ Avoid packing sweet treats, such as chocolate, pastries or cakes, or make them occasional rather than everyday items.

- ✓ Good lunch box alternatives to sugary food and potato crisps include yoghurt, fromage frais, rice pudding or custard; fruit scones, banana bread, dried fruit rolls and bars, fruit muffins; muesli bars, low-fat crisps, popcorn and pretzels.
- ✓ Always pack a bottle of water in addition to a diluted fruit juice drink, low-fat plain or flavoured milk, soy milk or vegetable juice.

Another important tip is to remember the value of leftovers: packing these can save time and energy, and kids love them. When planning for dinner, consider how you might incorporate leftovers into a lunch for the following day, then make a few extra servings and set them aside - for example, boiled eggs or omelette; chicken drumsticks or nuggets; healthy pizza slices; pasta or noodle dishes for snacks or salads; and roasted meat and vegetables for sandwich fillings.

Importantly, these easy to prepare healthy suggestions don't just apply to school or work lunches. They are just as good at home or packed for family outings like weekend picnics and hikes – for both children and adults alike.

Healthy sandwich, roll, pitta pocket and wrap fillings for children of different ages:

✓ Tuna or salmon with egg, lettuce and low-fat mayonnaise

✓ Roast beef, lamb or pork with tomato, low-fat cheese and lettuce

✓ Low-fat cream cheese, grated carrot, sliced capsicum and hummus

✓ Ricotta or cottage cheese, tuna and snow pea sprouts or baby spinach

✓ Avocado, low-fat cheese, tomato and bean sprouts

✓ Lean ham, lettuce, low-fat cheese and fruit chutney

✓ Low-fat cream cheese, baby spinach and roasted vegetables

✓ Mashed curried egg, cucumber, cheese and lettuce

✓ Chopped skinless chicken, low-fat mayonnaise, tomato and lettuce

✓ Tabouli salad, lettuce and feta cheese

✓ Peanut butter and jam

✓ Bananas mashed with ricotta cheese

✓ Hummus, sliced tomato, low-fat cheese and sprouts

✓ Home-made meat or fish rissoles sliced with tomato, lettuce and mustard

✓ Lean bacon, sliced egg, lettuce and avocado

✓ Sun dried tomatoes, sliced or roasted mushrooms, low-fat cheese and lettuce

✓ Vegemite and cheese

✓ Cream cheese or cottage cheese with honey or diced pineapple

✓ Cold baked beans or bean salad with lettuce, tomato and grated cheese

✓ Omelette, tomato and lettuce with mustard or chutney

Nutritious lunch box snacks and fillers:

✓ Fresh fruit, available in many varieties all year

✓ Vegetable sticks spread with a little peanut butter or low-fat cream cheese

✓ Reduced fat pretzels or popcorn

✓ Small container of yoghurt, rice pudding or custard

✓ Crackers, plain or with peanut butter or cheese

✓ Reduced fat cheese sticks

✓ Small zip-lock bag of dried fruit or nuts (not recommended for young children)

✓ Tortilla chips or bread sticks with a small tub of salsa, guacamole, or hummus

✓ Corn on the cob (without butter)

✓ Cold pancake or 2-3 pikelets plain or spread with jam

✓ Slice of fruit bread or pumpkin bread

✓ Banana bread

✓ Unsweetened muesli bars and fruit rolls

✓ Fruit or savoury muffins

✓ Salad snack container, for example mixed leaf salad, tabouli, pasta, bean or rice

✓ Mini quiches or a slice of frittata

✓ Small container of jelly or fruit in natural fruit juice

✓ Home-made pizza slice

✓ Chicken drumstick or home-made nuggets

✓ Fruit kebabs

Remember, it's important to keep food fresh so that it doesn't spoil. Wrap sandwiches in plastic wrap or put in snap-lock bags. Buy a lunch box with a water bottle that can be frozen the night before and packed to help keep food cold in hot weather. Alternatively, freeze small packs of milk or fruit juice - they will thaw out by lunchtime.

RECIPES

PREPARATION TIME
10 minutes
Makes 4 servings

STORAGE
Keep up to 5 days in an airtight container.

Fruity Snack Bags

½ cup mixed dried mango pieces, banana chips, apple and sultanas
¼ cup mixed nuts and seeds (older children only)
½ cup coconut shavings
½ cup plain toasted oats

Mix all ingredients together, then divide into small zip-lock bags.

Banana Bread

PREPARATION TIME

90 minutes

Makes 1 loaf or
12 slices

STORAGE

Allow to cool before
serving. Refrigerate in
an airtight container
for up to 4 days.
Great to freeze!

1 cup plain flour
2 tsp. baking powder
½ tsp. bicarbonate of soda
½ cup melted unsalted butter

¾ cup brown sugar
2 large eggs
4 large ripe bananas, mashed
1 tsp. vanilla extract

Preheat oven to 180°C.
Lightly oil a loaf tin and line with baking paper.
Mix together flour, baking powder and soda.
In a separate bowl, combine the butter and
sugar, then mix in the eggs, bananas and
vanilla extract until well blended.
Gradually add the flour mix, stirring well.
Pour into the tin and bake for 60-70 minutes
until golden brown, or until a skewer inserted
into the bread comes out clean.
Allow to cool. Serve plain or lightly spread
with peanut butter, cream cheese or other
healthy spreads.

Zucchini Fritters

PREPARATION TIME

20 minutes

Makes 20 fritters

STORAGE

Great hot or cold.
May be frozen and
reheated for tasty
teenage snacks
and veggie burgers.

2 cups grated zucchini (courgettes)
2 eggs
1 small onion, diced
½ cup grated low-fat cheese
½ cup plain flour
½ tsp. baking powder
1 vegetable stock cube, crushed

Mix together the zucchini, eggs, onion and cheese.
Add the flour, baking powder and stock cube mixed with a little water.
Spoon portions into a lightly oiled frying pan and cook on medium-high heat for 5 minutes, turning
once, until golden brown on both sides.
Serve in sandwiches or as a snack with hummus and lemon wedges.

Tasty Tortilla Crisps

PREPARATION TIME

10-15 minutes

Makes 1-2 servings for
kids or 1 for adults

STORAGE

Refrigerate in an
airtight container
for up to 2-3 days.

2 large flour tortillas
1 tbsp. light olive oil or cooking spray

½ tsp. mixed herbs or a handful of
grated parmesan to season (optional)

Preheat oven to 200°C. Lightly brush or spray
tortillas with oil, then cut each one into 8-10
wedges (try animal shaped biscuit cutters for
little kids). Arrange on a large baking tray.
Sprinkle with herbs or parmesan, if using.
Bake for 8-10 minutes until golden and crisp,
checking often. Allow to cool. Serve plain or
with dips or use for healthy nachos.

SPEEDY DINNER DELIGHTS

Dinner is an important part of any family's nutritional plan. Eating together at the end of the day provides quality time for you and your family to touch base, and an opportunity for you to model and encourage healthy eating habits. For busy families, the key to success is to enlist the help of the whole family, from meal planning, grocery shopping, and helping to prepare dinner to cleaning up afterwards. This collaborative effort helps take the load off busy parents and ensures the family meal is both nutritious and something everyone will enjoy.

Here are some balanced, easy to prepare dinner suggestions to try at home. Be sure to serve with some salad, rice or bread; a glass of water, low-fat milk or diluted fruit juice, and a piece of fruit.

There are 4-5 weeks of healthy family meal suggestions below. With the exception of the bakes and curries, most of the meals take between 20-30 minutes to prepare and cook. Mix and match these meal ideas for many more nutritious combinations:

Beef and Lamb*

- ✓ Lean minced beef tacos with roasted vegetables, fresh baby spinach, diced tomato and grated cheese. Serve with a piece of fresh watermelon.
- ✓ Lean beef or lamb strips, stir-fried with broccoli, mushrooms, snow peas, pumpkin, garlic, basil, coriander and soy. Serve with boiled or steamed rice.
- ✓ Home-made lean beefburgers on a warmed multigrain bun with avocado, mixed lettuce, tomato, low-fat cheese, bean sprouts and chutney. Serve with baked paprika potato wedges.
- ✓ Spaghetti bolognaise with lean ground beef, fresh tomatoes, mushrooms, baby spinach, garlic and oregano. Serve with grated parmesan cheese and a side salad.
- ✓ Grilled rump steak with mashed potato, steamed carrot and peas, blanched asparagus and a low-fat mushroom gravy.
- ✓ Grilled lamb and vegetable kebabs with chunks of marinated lean lamb, pineapple, zucchini (courgette), squash, cherry tomatoes and onion. Serve with a Greek salad and bread roll.
- ✓ Roast lamb with baked baby potatoes, whole baby carrots, eggplant, blanched green beans and a caramelized onion gravy.

*Enjoy 3 meals of beef or lamb a week as a good source of iron and protein; or equivalent alternatives for vegetarians.

Chicken and Pork

- ✓ Chicken and cheese tortellini pasta with diced snow peas and mushroom. Serve with a mixed leaf salad and fresh fruit.
- ✓ Roast organic chicken with stuffing and gravy. Serve with mashed potato, peas and corn on the cob (remove chicken skin before serving).
- ✓ Grilled marinated chicken breast or pork cutlets, served with paprika potato wedges and salad.
- ✓ Chicken strip burritos with a spring onion, asparagus, baby spinach, diced tomato and mushroom filling. Wrap and bake with a light topping of low-fat cheese. Serve with a bean salad.
- ✓ Chicken and vegetable noodle soup served with sweet corn fritters, crusty bread and hummus.
- ✓ Grilled chicken pieces allowed to cool, served over the top of a mixed leaf salad with croutons, parmesan cheese, lean bacon, boiled or poached egg, and low-fat Caesar dressing or vinaigrette. Serve with a bread roll.
- ✓ Honey and soy marinated chicken or pork kebabs with pineapple, onion and whole baby mushrooms, served with vegetable fried rice.
- ✓ Home-made chicken nuggets and a garden salad, served with a bread roll and chutney, low-fat mayonnaise or hummus for dipping.

Fish and Seafood**

- ✓ Steamed fresh fish fillets with soy, ginger and garlic, served with stir-fried vegetables and steamed rice.
- ✓ Grilled fish fillets with mashed potato, blanched carrot strips and asparagus. Serve with lemon wedges and low-fat mayonnaise.
- ✓ Stir-fried prawns or calamari with broccoli, snow peas, mushrooms, carrot and noodles in garlic, ginger and soy. Serve with fresh fruit.
- ✓ Fish fillet curry with sweet potato, mushrooms and baby spinach. Serve with plain rice and poppadoms.
- ✓ Wonton fish soup with cubed fish pieces, prawns, mushrooms, snow peas, corn and noodles or dumplings. Serve with rye crackers and fresh fruit.
- ✓ Home-made crumbed fish fingers with a vegetable pasta salad, and low-fat mayonnaise, hummus or tomato chutney for dipping.
- ✓ Prawn, snow pea and basil pesto pasta served with a Greek salad and bread roll.
- ✓ Salmon fish cakes made with tinned salmon, potatoes, chives, parsley, dill and mayonnaise, rolled in breadcrumbs and baked. Serve with lemon wedges, dipping sauce and a side salad.

**Enjoy at least 1-2 meals of fish a week as a good source of omega-3 fats.

Vegetarian

- Lasagne of baby spinach, mushroom, kidney beans, tomato and pumpkin, topped with tomato sauce and cheese. Serve with a mixed leaf salad.
- Winter vegetable soup of leek, potato, mushroom, and corn. Serve with rice cakes or sweetcorn fritters.
- Pizza with a garlic and oregano tomato base, topped with cherry or sun-dried tomatoes, mushrooms, snow peas, olives and low-fat ricotta or mozzarella cheese. Serve with salad and fruit.
- Ricotta and spinach cannelloni with a fresh tomato sauce of garlic, basil and mushroom, served with a rocket and avocado salad.
- Stir-fried marinated tofu with broccoli, snow peas, mushrooms, spring onion, garlic, ginger and soy. Serve with plain rice or noodles.
- Lentil and cheese burger on a wholegrain bun with fresh salad greens, tomato and mustard or chutney. Serve with paprika potato wedges.
- Yellow vegetable curry of pumpkin, potato, mushroom, lentils, and broccoli served with poppadoms or rye crackers and fresh melon.
- Omelette or quiche with mushroom, asparagus, crushed cherry tomato, baby spinach and shredded low-fat cheese. Serve with a side salad and bread roll.

Salads and sides

- Garden salad of mixed lettuce leaves, baby spinach, cherry tomatoes, snow peas, carrot sticks and cucumber. Serve with vinaigrette or desired low-fat dressing and a toasted muffin with hummus.
- Caesar salad of cos lettuce, lean grilled bacon strips, low-fat parmesan cheese, home-made multigrain croutons, and poached egg. Serve with a low-fat Caesar dressing and fresh bread roll.

- Greek salad of cucumber slices, red capsicum, reduced fat feta cheese, tomato wedges or cherry tomatoes, spring onion and black olives. Serve with a vinaigrette and pizza bread sticks.
- Rocket, avocado, snow pea, and shaved parmesan salad tossed with grilled pine nuts (not suitable for small children). Serve with a vinaigrette and wholegrain pappadams.
- Three bean salad of kidney beans, chickpeas, and blanched green beans tossed with baby spinach, diced cherry tomatoes, feta cheese, lemon juice, balsamic vinegar, and brown sugar. Serve with home-made tortilla chips and salsa.
- New potato salad with sliced egg and flaked tuna tossed in a yoghurt, mayonnaise, wholegrain mustard and chive dressing. Serve with rye bread.
- Three colour pasta spiral salad with blanched vegetables and cherry tomatoes tossed in a dressing of shaved parmesan cheese, parsley, lemon juice, mustard and balsamic vinegar.
- Sweetcorn fritters made from wholegrain flour, egg, spring onion, coriander, pepper and sweet corn. Great served with soup and salad.

When preparing and serving dinner, be mindful of the ideal plate, and the importance of balancing the food groups and appropriate portion sizes. Remember that healthy preparation and cooking methods are also important, since poor cooking methods can spoil even the best food, leaching nutrients or adding unwanted fat and kilojoules. If you have leftovers or plan ahead and make extra for lunches and snacks the next day, make sure you store food correctly to avoid spoiling.

For these and other recipes visit www.abcfitkids.com/recipes for free downloadable recipe sheets and meal planners.

RECICES

Lean Beef Tacos

PREPARATION TIME

20 minutes

Makes 8 tacos

STORAGE

Best served
immediately.

1 cup three bean mix
2 large tomatoes, diced
1 tbsp. crushed garlic
1 tbsp. mixed herbs (paprika, basil, black pepper)

1 cup lean beef mince
8 taco shells
grated low-fat cheese
shredded lettuce and diced tomato

Heat a little olive oil in a frying pan. Cook the bean mix, tomatoes, garlic and herbs over medium heat for 5 minutes. Add the mince and simmer for 5-10 minutes until the mixture is dry.
Meanwhile, heat the taco shells in a warm oven.
Sprinkle grated cheese over the top of the bean mixture and turn off the heat.
Scoop several spoonfuls of bean mix into each taco and top with shredded lettuce and tomato.
Serve with a bean or mixed salad, side of salsa and fresh fruit.

Tasty Chicken Nuggets

PREPARATION TIME

15 minutes

Makes 20 nuggets

STORAGE

Best served
immediately. Keep
refrigerated for 2
days. Great to freeze!

2 lean chicken breasts
1 cup breadcrumbs
½ tsp. chicken or vegetable stock powder

1 egg
¼ cup low-fat milk
plain flour

Cut the chicken into bite-sized pieces. Preheat the oven to 180°C.
Put the breadcrumbs in a flat bowl.
Mix the stock powder, egg and milk in another flat bowl. Sprinkle flour in another bowl.
Roll the chicken pieces in flour, then coat with egg mixture, then breadcrumbs.
Place chicken nuggets evenly on baking tray.
Bake for 10-15 minutes until golden brown on both sides.
Serve with pasta salad or vegetables, bread and hummus or low-fat mayonnaise.

Marinated Baked Fish Fillets

PREPARATION TIME

30-40 minutes

4-5 servings

STORAGE

Best served
immediately.

4 medium fish fillets
3 spring onions, chopped
2 tbsp. runny honey
1 tbsp. crushed garlic
1 tbsp. dried basil

1 tbsp. grated fresh ginger
1 tbsp. olive oil
¼ cup hot water
2 tbsp. soy sauce
12 cherry tomatoes

Preheat oven to 200°C.
Arrange fish in a lightly oiled large baking dish.
Mix together spring onions, honey, garlic, basil, ginger, olive oil, water and soy.
Pour mixture evenly over fish and leave to stand for 10 minutes.
Garnish with cherry tomatoes and bake in the oven for 25-30 minutes.
Serve with mashed potato, blanched carrot strips and asparagus, lemon wedges and low-fat mayonnaise.

Vegetarian Pizza

PREPARATION TIME

15-20 minutes

Makes 1 pizza

STORAGE

Best served
immediately.

plain pizza base or Lebanese bread
⅓ cup tomato pasta sauce
1 tsp. crushed garlic
1 tsp. mixed herbs (oregano and basil)

sliced mushroom, sun-dried tomatoes,
    diced spring onion, black pitted olives,
    blanched snow peas
grated low-fat mozzarella cheese

Preheat oven to 180°C. Put pizza base on tray.
Combine pasta sauce, garlic and herbs and spread
over base.
Add toppings and sprinkle lightly with cheese.
Place in oven and cook for 10-15 minutes until
cheese begins to crisp and turn golden brown.
Serve with a mixed salad and some fruit.

Roast Chicken Noodle Soup

PREPARATION TIME

40 minutes

Makes 1 litre

STORAGE

Best served
immediately.
Keep refrigerated for
1-2 days. Great to
freeze, before you add
the pasta.

roast chicken leftovers
3 spring onions, chopped
2 chicken stock cubes
1 tbsp. crushed garlic

1 medium sweet potato, diced
1 carrot, chopped
1 small can corn kernels
thin spaghetti, broken into smaller lengths

Remove skin and meat from chicken carcass. Chop meat and set aside. Put carcass in a large
saucepan with the spring onion, crushed stock cubes and garlic.
Add water to cover the carcass by 2.5 cm, then bring to boil and let simmer for 30 minutes. Drain,
reserving the stock and discarding the carcass. Return the stock to the clean pan and add the sweet
potato, carrot and corn. Simmer for another 10 minutes, then add the spaghetti pieces and chicken
meat and cook until the spaghetti is tender. Pour into bowls, garnish with bean sprouts and serve
with corn fritters and crusty bread.

Lamb & Vegetable Kebabs

PREPARATION TIME

20 minutes

Makes 8-10 kebabs

STORAGE

Best served
immediately. Keep
refrigerated for 1-2
days. Great to freeze!

440 g can pineapple slices in juice
pinch of black pepper
1 garlic clove, crushed
1 tbsp. chopped coriander
1 tbsp. soy sauce
400 g lean lamb, diced

Drain pineapple pieces and mix ¼ cup of the
juice with the pepper, garlic, coriander and soy.
Thread the lamb, pineapple and vegetables on
8-10 skewers and place in a shallow
baking dish.
Coat with the sauce and place under a preheated
medium-high grill, turning frequently,
for 10-15 minutes until cooked through.
Serve with a fresh Greek salad and bread.

8-10 mushrooms, halved
1 large brown onion, quartered
punnet of cherry tomatoes
1 zucchini (courgette), diced
8-10 squash, halved

Salmon Fish Cakes

PREPARATION TIME

30 minutes

Makes 12 fish cakes

STORAGE

Best served immediately. Keep refrigerated for 1-2 days. Great to freeze!

2 cups mashed potato
500 g can pink salmon or tuna in
 springwater, drained
2 tbsp. chopped chives
1 tbsp. chopped dill

2 tbsp. mayonnaise
juice of half a lemon
1 egg
plain flour and breadcrumbs, to coat
1 egg, mixed with ¼ cup milk

Preheat the oven to 220°C.
Mix together the mashed potato, salmon, chives, dill, mayonnaise, lemon juice and egg. Make into 12 round cakes.
Roll the fish cakes in flour, then coat with egg and milk mixture, then roll in the breadcrumbs. Arrange the cakes on a lightly oiled tray, flatten and bake for 20-25 minutes, turning once, until golden brown on both sides.
Serve with lemon wedges and a salad.

Greek Salad

PREPARATION TIME

5-10 minutes

4 servings

STORAGE

Best served immediately.

mixed lettuce leaves
1 large tomato, cut into wedges
1 small Spanish onion, sliced
1 cucumber, diced
½ red capsicum (pepper), diced

pitted black olives
low-fat feta cheese, cubed
juice of 1 lemon
3 tbsp. olive oil
3 tbsp. balsamic vinegar

Toss together the lettuce, tomato, Spanish onion, cucumber, capsicum, olives and feta cheese. Whisk together the lemon juice, olive oil and vinegar to make a dressing for the salad.
Serve with bread sticks and some fruit.

Vegetable Lasagne

PREPARATION TIME

50 minutes

4-5 servings

STORAGE

Best served immediately. Keep refrigerated for 1-2 days. Great to freeze!

1 large onion, diced
1 zucchini (courgette), diced
1 can lentils, drained
2 tomatoes, diced
6-8 mushrooms, diced

1 tbsp. crushed garlic
1 tbsp. mixed dried herbs
1 packet lasagne sheets
1 jar tomato pasta sauce
1 cup low-fat ricotta cheese
½ cup low-fat mozzarella cheese

Preheat oven to 180°C.
Heat a splash of olive oil in a pan and fry the onion, zucchini, lentils, tomatoes, mushrooms, garlic and herbs until soft.
Arrange a layer of lasagne sheets in a greased baking dish, then layer with pasta sauce and top with the vegetable mix and a layer of crumbled ricotta. Repeat until there are 3 layers of vegetable and ricotta mix, then add a layer of lasagne sheets and top with pasta sauce and grated mozzarella.
Cook for 40-45 minutes, until pasta is cooked.
Serve with a mixed salad and some fruit.

MARVELLOUS MUNCHIES, SNACKS AND DESSERTS

Snacks are an important part of a balanced nutrition plan, and make up the smaller meals both children and adults need in between breakfast, lunch and dinner. Often though, with so many convenience foods available, snack times can be a challenge. On the one hand snacks can be a beneficial addition to the daily nutrition plan and a way of satisfying serving recommendations from the different important food groups. On the other, poor snack selections such as sweets and crisps can add excess energy and interfere with a child's appetite at the next meal.

One way to improve the picture is to substitute easy, healthy snacks for the usual options. Here are some healthy substitutions that your child probably won't even notice:

Crisps and Chips
- Popcorn
- Pretzels
- Breadsticks
- Tortilla chips
- Rice crackers
- Baked potato wedges
- Vegetable sticks spread with peanut butter
- Dry cereal or trail mix
- Cheese-on-toast fingers
- Corn on the cob

Chocolate, Sugary Sweets, Cakes and Biscuits
- Offer chocolate with a higher cocoa content and dark chocolate in smaller portions
- Fresh, tinned and dried fruits
- Handful of chocolate coated nuts (not suitable for small children)
- Strawberries or banana dipped in melted chocolate or hazelnut spread
- Caramelized apples
- Home-made brownies
- Fruit and savoury muffins
- Carrot cake
- Banana cake with yoghurt icing
- Fruit loaf or scones

- Pancakes and pikelets
- Healthy muesli bars with fruit, nuts and chocolate chips
- Yoghurt bars
- Choc chip oatmeal cookies
- Rice cakes with cream cheese and honey

Ice Cream and Desserts
- Low-fat ice cream varieties with fruit
- Sorbet
- Soy desserts and ice creams
- Frozen fruits on a stick rolled in coconut shavings
- Low-fat frozen yoghurts
- Natural unsweetened icy poles and fruit poppers
- Home-made flavoured milk ice treats
- Low-fat custards and rice puddings
- Low-fat thickened yoghurt varieties with fruit or honey and cinnamon
- Jelly with fruit
- Banana split with strawberries, honey and a small scoop of ice cream
- Fruit crepes with a dollop of frozen yoghurt and a light dusting of icing sugar
- Low-fat cheesecake varieties with a fruit glaze
- Healthy fruit and yoghurt smoothies

Sweetened Drinks

✓ Fruit juice spritzers

✓ Milkshakes with low-fat milk or calcium- enriched soymilk (use fruit to flavour for banana and strawberry or moderate amounts of syrup or powder for chocolate and caramel)

✓ Healthy fruit smoothies

✓ Fruit juice (preferably diluted)

✓ Iced still or sparkling mineral water with citrus fruit wedges

✓ Healthy hot chocolate

Importantly, choose varieties low in fat, sugar and salt when buying pretzels, popcorn, muesli bars, and ice-cream substitutes. Keep portion sizes small, and have desserts and snacks that include chocolate as occasional treats 1-2 times a week, or on special occasions. Snacks such as fruit, yoghurts, home-made muesli bars, banana bread, muffins and vegetable sticks are always the best choice.

RECIPES

Paprika Potato Wedges

PREPARATION TIME

10-15 minutes

STORAGE

Best served immediately.

4 large potatoes, washed or peeled
1 tsp. paprika
4 tbsp. olive oil

1 tbsp. crushed garlic
1 tsp. dried oregano or basil

Preheat oven to 220°C.
Cut potatoes into wedges.
Mix paprika, oil, garlic and herbs together in a large bowl.
Toss the potato wedges in the oil and herb mixture until well coated.
Spread wedges evenly in a large baking tray.
Cook for 40-50 minutes, turning occasionally until crisp and brown.
Serve plain or with healthy dips or chutneys.

Chocolate Nut Brownies

PREPARATION TIME

30 minutes
Makes 20-25 brownies

STORAGE

Refrigerate in an airtight container for 3-4 days.

¾ cup plain chocolate
¾ cup butter
3 large eggs
1 cup caster sugar

1 tsp. vanilla extract
½ cup plain flour
½ cup chopped hazelnuts

Preheat oven to 180°C.
Melt chocolate and butter together in the microwave.
Beat together the eggs, sugar and vanilla, then add chocolate mixture.
Mix in the flour and nuts and then transfer to a 20 cm square cake tin lined with baking paper.
Bake for 20-25 minutes, then cool in the tin for 10 minutes.
Cut into squares and allow to cool completely before removing from tin.

Honey and Cinnamon Yoghurt

PREPARATION TIME

15 minutes plus
freezing time

STORAGE

Keeps refrigerated
for 3-4 days.

1 litre full cream milk
1 cup powdered milk
4 tbsp. plain natural yoghurt

3 tbsp. honey
1 tbsp. cinnamon

Simmer milk and milk powder on medium-low
heat in a saucepan.
Pour into a large glass jar and allow to cool.
When the milk is lukewarm, mix in the yoghurt.
Place lid on the jar and wrap in a blanket and
let stand in a warm spot overnight (under your
child's bed is perfect!).
Refrigerate the next morning and then stir in
the honey and cinnamon. Serve plain or with
berries or stewed apples or pears.

Baked Cheesecake

PREPARATION TIME

40-50 minutes
Makes 1 cake

STORAGE

Keeps for 2-3 days in
the fridge. Suitable for
freezing.

¼ cup butter, melted
⅔ cup sweet wholemeal
**   biscuit crumbs**

2 eggs
¾ cup caster sugar
1 tsp. vanilla extract
500 g cream cheese

Preheat oven to 180°C.
Mix melted butter with biscuit crumbs.
Press biscuit mix into the base of a 20 cm
round springform tin.
Beat together the eggs, sugar, vanilla extract
and cream cheese. Pour over biscuit base.
Bake for 30 minutes or until just set. Turn oven
off, prop door ajar and leave cheesecake in
oven to cool completely.
Serve cold with strawberries.

Fruit Juice Spritzer

PREPARATION TIME

10 minutes
Makes 1 serving

STORAGE

Serve immediately.

ice
orange, grapefruit or apple juice
lemon and lime wedges
2 strawberries
3-4 mint leaves
sparkling mineral water

Put ice and a straw in a tall glass.
Pour in fruit juice until 1/3 full.
Add 2-3 citrus wedges, halved strawberries
and mint leaves.
Top up with mineral water, stirring gently.

Oatmeal Peanut Butter Biscuits

PREPARATION TIME

30 minutes

Makes 40 cookies

STORAGE

Allow to cool before serving. Store in an airtight container for up to 4 days. Great to freeze!

3 tbsp. butter
½ cup crunchy peanut butter
½ cup sugar
½ cup firmly packed brown sugar

2 large eggs
1 tsp. vanilla extract
1 cup plain flour
1 tsp. baking powder
2 cups rolled oats

Preheat oven to 180°C.
Cream together butter, peanut butter and sugars.
Add eggs and vanilla extract and beat well.
Add flour, baking powder and a pinch of salt.
Mix together, then stir in the oats.
Lightly grease a large baking tray and, using a spoon, place small portions of dough about 5 cm apart.
Bake for 10-15 minutes until biscuits are firm.
Remove biscuits with a spatula and cool on a wire rack.
Serve 1-2 biscuits with a glass of low-fat milk.

Super Strawberry Smoothie

PREPARATION TIME

5 minutes

Makes 1 serving

STORAGE

Best served immediately.

4 large strawberries
½ medium banana
⅓ cup plain yoghurt
½ cup low-fat milk
1 tbsp. coconut shavings

Wash strawberries thoroughly.
Blend fruit and yoghurt together until smooth.
Add milk and coconut and blend until frothy.
Serve in a tall glass with ice and a straw.

Quick and Easy Apple Crumble

PREPARATION TIME

10-15 minutes

STORAGE

Great hot or cold. Refrigerate in an airtight container for 3-4 days. Great to freeze!

4 cooking apples
½ tsp. ground nutmeg
¼ tsp. ground cinnamon
3 tbsp. water

2 tbsp. cold butter
¼ cup self-raising flour
4 tbsp. brown sugar
2 tbsp. desiccated coconut
2 tbsp. rolled oats

Preheat oven to 200°C.
Peel, core and slice apples.
Place in a large ovenproof dish with nutmeg, cinnamon and water.
Rub butter into flour until mixture is crumbly and then mix in the brown sugar, coconut and rolled oats.
Sprinkle over apples and bake in oven for 25-30 minutes until top is golden.
Allow to cool, and serve with a glass of low-fat milk or with yoghurt.

Breakfast  **Lunch** **Dinner**

A WEEK OF WINTER MEAL IDEAS

Monday

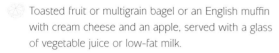 Toasted fruit or multigrain bagel or an English muffin with cream cheese and an apple, served with a glass of vegetable juice or low-fat milk.

Chicken noodle soup in a wide mouth thermos with a bread roll.
Small tin of fruit salad, muesli bar, rye crackers with cheese, juice popper.

Winter vegetable soup with leek, potato, mushroom, and corn. Serve with rice cakes or sweet corn fritters.

Tuesday

Microwaved porridge with fresh or dried fruit. Serve with low-fat milk or soy milk and a glass of diluted apple juice.

Pitta pocket with cottage cheese, tuna, roasted vegetables and baby spinach
Apple, fruit muffin, bag of pretzels, carton of milk.

 Chicken strip burritos with a spring onion, asparagus, baby spinach, diced tomato and mushroom filling. Wrap and bake with a light topping of low-fat cheese. Serve with a warm bean salad.

Wednesday

Low-fat savoury or fruit muffin, warmed in the microwave, served with fruit and a glass of low-fat milk or soy milk.

Lean ham sandwich on multigrain with lettuce, low-fat cheese and fruit chutney.
Banana, yoghurt, tortilla chips or bread sticks, vegetable juice.

Grilled rump steak with mashed potato, steamed carrot and peas, blanched asparagus and a low-fat mushroom gravy.

Thursday

Yoghurt with sliced fruit and toast with hummus. Serve with a glass of vegetable juice, low-fat milk or calcium-enriched soy milk.

 Low-fat cream cheese, baby spinach and roasted veges.
Orange, chicken drumstick, custard, vanilla milk.

Stir-fried prawns with broccoli, snow peas, mushrooms, carrot and noodles with garlic, ginger and soy. Serve with fresh fruit.

Friday

Bowl of weetbix, bran flakes or corn flakes with low fat milk or soy milk, and diced, canned or stewed fruit. Serve with a glass of water or diluted fruit juice.

Chopped skinless chicken, low-fat mayonnaise, tomato and lettuce.
Apple, vegetable sticks with peanut butter, rice pudding, juice popper.

Home-made lean beef burgers on a warmed multigrain bun with avocado, mixed lettuce, tomato, low-fat cheese, bean sprouts and chutney. Serve with a side of baked paprika potato wedges.

Saturday

Breakfast burrito with scrambled egg, tomato, grated cheese, diced ham or other favourite ingredients. Serve with a glass of diluted fruit juice.

Home-made crumbed fish fingers with a vegetable pasta salad, and low-fat mayonnaise, hummus or tomato chutney for dipping.
Fruit kebabs, popcorn, oatmeal peanut butter biscuits and milk.

Yellow vegetable curry of pumpkin, potato, mushroom, lentils, and broccoli served with pappadams or rye crackers and fresh melon.

Sunday

Low-fat pancakes with fresh fruit and a light drizzling of honey or a little brown sugar. Serve with a glass of water or vegetable juice.

Omelette, tomato and lettuce with mustard or chutney.
Fruit and yoghurt, pizza slice, hot chocolate.

Roast organic chicken with stuffing and gravy. Serve with mashed potato, peas and corn on the cob (remove chicken skin before serving).

Always include a bottle of water with packed lunches.

Serve dinner with a glass of water or diluted fruit juice. A jug of iced water with citrus wedges in the middle of the table is a great idea. LImit after-dinner treats or desserts to one or two nights a week such as a midweek after dinner treat or a weekend family breakfast special.

A WEEK OF SUMMER MEAL IDEAS

Monday

Yoghurt with sliced fruit and toast with hummus. Serve with a glass of vegetable juice, low-fat milk or calcium-enriched soy milk.

Tuna pitta bread with egg, lettuce and low-fat mayonnaise. Apple, crackers with peanut butter, corn on the cob, juice popper.

Stir-fry lean beef strips with broccoli, mushrooms, snow peas, pumpkin, garlic, basil, coriander and soy. Serve with boiled or steamed rice.

Tuesday

Bowl of unsweetened muesli with grated apple or diced strawberries served with low-fat milk, plain yoghurt or soy milk and a glass of water.

Cream cheese sandwich with carrot, capsicum and hummus on multigrain bread. Small tin of fruit salad, bag of pretzels, muffin, carton of milk.

Honey and soy marinated chicken kebabs with pineapple, onion and whole baby mushrooms, served with vegetable fried rice.

Wednesday

Boiled egg with wholemeal toast soldiers. Serve with fresh fruit and a glass of low-fat milk or soy milk.

Lean ham bread roll with lettuce, tomato, low-fat cheese and fruit chutney. Banana, tub of yoghurt, muesli bar, vegetable juice.

Grilled fish fillets with mashed potato, blanched carrot strips and asparagus. Serve with lemon wedges and low-fat mayonnaise.

Thursday

Rice cakes spread with peanut butter and jam plus an apple. Serve with a glass of low-fat milk or soy milk.

Mashed curried egg sandwich with cucumber, cheese and lettuce. Strawberries, bread sticks and hummus, tub of custard, juice popper.

Lean ground beef tacos with roasted vegetables, fresh baby spinach, diced tomato and grated cheese. Serve with fresh watermelon.

Friday

Berry banana breakfast smoothie made from blended low-fat yoghurt or soy yoghurt, banana, strawberries, and whole grain cereal. Serve with a slice of toast or muffin.

Roast chicken wrap with baby spinach, pineapple, and cream cheese. Slice of banana bread, tub of jelly, dried fruit and nuts, chocolate milk.

Pizza with a garlic and oregano tomato base, topped with cherry or sun dried tomatoes, mushrooms, snow peas, olives and low-fat ricotta or mozzarella cheese. Serve with salad and fruit.

Saturday

French toast served with a slice of honeydew melon, a dollop of yoghurt and a glass of diluted orange juice or vegetable juice.

Home-made beef rissoles in a burger bun with tomato, lettuce and mustard. Slice of watermelon and a fruit juice spritzer.

Salmon fish cakes made with tinned salmon, potatoes, chives parsley, dill and mayonnaise, rolled in breadcrumbs and baked. Serve with lemon wedges, dipping sauce and a side salad.

Sunday

Omelette with diced mushroom, corn, baby spinach and low-fat grated cheese. Serve with rye crackers and a slice of water melon. Add a glass of water or diluted fruit juice.

Bean salad wrap with lettuce, tomato and grated cheese. Yoghurt with fruit and a glass of diluted apple juice.

Spaghetti bolognaise with lean beef mince, fresh tomatoes, mushrooms, baby spinach, garlic and oregano. Serve topped with grated parmesan cheese, salad and a bread roll.

Helpful Resources

Useful links to more information about child development, nutrition and fitness, parenting help, emotional wellbeing and relationship building

ABC Fit Kids**
→ www.abcfitkids.com

ABC Health Matters Website**
→ www.abc.net.au/health

Allergy Information**
→ www.allergyfacts.org.au

Australian Breast Feeding Association**
→ www.breastfeeding.asn.au

Australian Childhood Foundation**
→ www.childhood.org.au

Australian Consumers Association Magazine**
→ www.choice.com.au

Australian Institute of Health & Welfare
→ www.aihw.gov.au

Australasian Society for the Study of Obesity
→ www.asso.org.au

Better Health Channel**
→ www.betterhealth.vic.gov.au

Cancer Council NSW**
→ www.cancercouncil.com.au

Child Accident Prevention Foundation**
→ www.kidsafe.com.au/

Australian Department of Health and Aging
→ www.health.gov.au

Diabetes Australia**
→ www.diabetesaustralia.com.au

Dietitians Association of Australia**
→ www.daa.asn.au

Eating Disorders Foundation of Victoria
→ www.eatingdisorders.org.au

Family Services Australia
→ www.fsa.org.au

Food Australia
→ www.foodaust.com.au

Food Safety Information
→ www.foodsafety.asn.au

Food Standards Australia New Zealand**
→ www.foodstandards.gov.au

Healthy Active Initiative**
→ www.healthyactive.gov.au

Health NSW Active Kids Site**
→ www.health.nsw.gov.au/obesity/youth

Heart Foundation**
→ www.heartfoundation.com.au

Kids Count**
→ www.kidscount.com.au

Kids Help Line
→ www.kidshelp.com.au

Lifeline Australia**
→ www.lifeline.org.au

Medical Journal of Australia
→ www.mja.com.au

My Doctor**
→ www.mydr.com.au

National Asthma Council of Australia**
→ www.nationalasthma.org.au

National Health & Medical Research Council
→ www.nhmrc.gov.au

Nutrition Australia**
→ www.nutritionaustralia.org

Parenting Blog Online**
→ www.theparentingblog.org

Public Health Association of Australia
→ www.phaa.net.au

Raising Children Network**
→ www.raisingchildren.net.au

Relationship Support and Insight**
→ www.relate.gov.au/

Relationships Australia
→ www.relationships.com.au

Royal Australian College of General Practitioners
→ www.racgp.org.au

Royal Children's Hospital Melbourne
→ www.rch.org.au/ecconnections/parents

Sudden Infant Death Syndrome
→ www.sidsandkids.org

Sydney Children's Hospital Fact Sheets
→ www.sch.edu.au/health/factsheets

Sports Dietitians Association of Australia
→ www.sportsdietitians.com

Weight Management Council
→ www.weightcouncil.org

Westmead Children's Hospital Kids Health Links**
→ www.chw.edu.au/parents/kidshealth

**highly recommended sites

Index

Please note: recipes are listed together under *recipes*.

A

acne 27
activity 5, 34, 82
    age-appropriate 82-5
    benefits 82-3
    in daily life 86-7
    non-traditional 85
    rainy days 87
    traditional 84-5
activity needs
    0-2 years 18, 83
    2-5 years 21, 84
    5-12 years 24, 84-5
    12-18 years 26-7, 84-5
additives 42-3, 47, 78
ADHD 44
adolescence 23, 24, 32, 67
advertising 5, 11, 23, 74-5
alcohol 26
allergic reactions 17, 40-1
anaphylaxis 40
antioxidants 42, 53
anxiety 24-5, 40
    and exercise 47
appetite 16, 18, 21
arthritis 12
asthma 6, 40, 43
    and exercise 47
    and food intolerance 42
attention disorders 6, 40, 44-5
    and exercise 47
    and food intolerance 42

B

babies 16-19
bed-wetting 25
Best Before date 79
beverages 66-71, 119
birth weight, low 12
body fat 30
body image 26, 27, 30
body mass index (BMI) 31
bone density 23
boundaries 23, 25-6
brain development 18
bread 50-1
breakfast 106
    5-minute ideas 106
    recipes 106-8
breastfeeding 12, 17

C

caffeine 45, 70
calcium 55, 78
car use 26, 86
carbohydrates 50-1
cardiovascular problems 6, 12
cereals 50-1
change 100
    finding motivation 37
    introducing slowly 35-6, 102-3
    keys to success 36

child development 16
    0-2 years 16-19
    2-5 years 20-2
    5-12 years 22-5
    12-18 years 25-7
childhood obesity *see* obesity
choking hazards 18
Cholesterol Free in labelling 76
chores 21, 24, 59, 86
cola drinks 70
communication 95-6, 100-1, 102
competition 21, 84-5
convenience foods 5, 10
cow's milk 42
cravings, dealing with 62-3, 88

D

dairy products 42, 55
    see also milk
dehydration 43-4, 66
dental care 21, 24
    and beverages 70-1
depression 12, 13, 40
    and exercise 47
desserts 118
developmental stages *see* child development
diabetes 12, 40
diet, changing 33, 35-6
dietary fibre *see* fibre
dieting 6, 26, 27, 35
digestive problems 12
dinner 112-14
    recipes 115-17
discouragement, avoiding 89
diuretics 44
down time 102
drink bottles 67
drugs 26

E

eating disorders 25, 27, 35
eating out 58-9
eating plan 63
emotional development 23
    0-2 years 16-17
    2-5 years 20
    5-12 years 23
    12-18 years 25-6
endurance/aerobic activities 83
energy drinks 66, 70
energy levels 6, 13, 21
energy needs 32-3
    assessing 32-3
exercise 5, 7, 23, 27
    around the house 86-7
    benefits of 47, 82-3
    lack of *see* sedentary pastimes
    types of 83
exploration, safe, for toddlers 83
eyeball test 30

F

fad diets 6, 10, 26
fair play 21

Index

family activities 6, 7, 13, 24, 37, 84-5, 93
family effort, required to make changes 6, 13, 100
family meals...95-6
family time 92-3, 100
fast food see convenience foods
fasting..26
fat
    and brain development 18
    consumption 5
    hidden 56
    requirements 33
Fat Free in labelling...75, 76
fibre...50, 68
fish..54, 113
fitness
    plan 89
    goals 87-8
flavour enhancers 42
flexibility activities 83
fluids 18, 44, 66
fluoride...71
food
    allowing children to serve themselves 21
    disguising..20, 62
    healthy choices....................................13, 59-61, 74, 97
    ideal plate 57
    solid 16
    storage methods...79
    unhealthy choices, eliminating 6-7, 45, 47, 102
food allergies 40-1, 78
food colourings 42, 43
food diary 32
food elimination program 45, 47
food groups..50-7
food intolerance 42-3, 78
food marketing 74-6
food refusal ....20-1, 21-2 see also fussy eaters
formula feeding 17
friendship 20, 24
fruit juice..68
fruits 10, 33
    food group..53
fun 37, 94, 95, 101
fussy eaters 21-2, 61-2
    dairy 55

G

games..21, 84
gardening...86
gender typing 20
Generation O 11
goals 37, 87-8
grains...50-1
growth see physical growth

H

health... 7, 100
health problems 5, 12
    see also individual topics
healthy eating plan 63
High in Calcium in labelling..75
hormones 23
    imbalance 12
hydration 18, 43-4, 66-7
hyperactivity 42, 43

I

ideal plate...57
impulse buying 74
incentives..88, 94
independence...25-6
infants 16-19, 32, 83
ingredients list...56, 68, 75, 76, 78
instant messaging...12
iron 17, 23

J

joint injuries 12
juice...68-9
junk food 7, 10

K

kilojoules 10, 32-3

L

labels
    on food 36, 41, 43, 56, 79
    see also ingredients list; nutritional information panels
lactose intolerance..42, 55, 67-8
legumes 54
lethargy 40, 42
    and exercise 47
Low-fat in labelling..75
lunch boxes 23, 58, 59
    contents 109-10
    recipes 110-11

M

meal times 95-6
meat 54, 56
    beef/lamb ideas..112
    chicken/pork ideas..113
media influence 5, 23, 25, 74
menstruation 27
menus 122-3
metabolism 21, 23
milk..55, 56, 67-8
minerals 50, 51, 74
mirror test 30
mobile phones..12
modelling 13, 21, 60, 92-3, 96
motivation 37, 93
    for kids 94, 100
    for parents 95, 101
MSG (monosodium glutamate)....................................43

N

napping...18, 20
No Added Sugar in labelling..75
nutrition 7, 16, 33
    food groups...50-7
nutritional information panels....................................36, 75-8
nutritional needs
    0-2 years...16-17, 55, 67
    2-5 years..20-1, 67
    5-12 years 23, 55, 67
    12-18 years 26, 67

O

obesity...5, 30
    causes 10-11
    and soft drinks 10

omega-3 fats..54
organic-certified produce..............................79
overeating...10
overweight...30
    causes 10-11

P

packaging..75
parenting...97
pasta...50-1
peanut allergy..41
peer pressure.................................23, 24, 25
peer relationships................................23, 26
physical activity *see* activity
physical education............................12, 24, 26
physical growth
    0-2 years..16
    2-5 years..20
    5-12 years...22-3
    12-18 years...25
pinch test..31
play..............................11, 21, 37, 82-4, 85
    benefits...101
portion sizes..58
praise, motivating through............................37
preschoolers...20-2, 84
preservatives....................................42, 43, 79
protein..23, 54
puberty..23, 27

R

rebellion...25-6
recipes
    apple crumble....................................121
    baked beans, home-made....................108
    banana bread.....................................111
    banana and coconut pancakes.............108
    biscuits, oatmeal peanut butter...........121
    breakfast bars....................................107
    brownies, chocolate nut.......................119
    cheesecake..120
    chicken nuggets.................................115
    fish fillets, baked................................115
    French toast triangles.........................108
    fruit cereal snack bags........................110
    fruit juice spritzers.............................120
    fruit muffins, low-fat..........................107
    Greek salad.......................................117
    honey and cinnamon yoghurt..............120
    lamb and vegetable kebabs.................116
    lean beef tacos..................................115
    paprika potato wedges.......................119
    porridge with dried fruit......................107
    roast chicken noodle soup...................116
    salmon fish cakes...............................117
    savoury muffins, low-fat......................107
    smoothie, strawberry..........................121
    tortilla crisps.....................................111
    vegetable lasagne..............................117
    vegetarian pizza.................................116
    zucchini fritters 111
Reduced Fat/Salt in labelling 75
rest, importance of.....................................102
restaurants...58-9
rewards...37, 88, 94
rice...50-1

Ritalin..44
role models............................13, 92-3, 96

S

salads/sides..114
school lunches *see* lunch boxes
sedentary pastimes.............5, 11, 24, 26-7, 82
sprucing up..87
self-esteem.....................12, 13, 25, 27, 37
separation anxiety.................................16-17, 24
sex, adolescent experimentation....................26
sexuality...27
shellfish..42
SIDS (Sudden Infant Death Syndrome)...........19
skin rashes..42
sleep..102
slimming *see* dieting
snacks...56, 118-19
social development..12
    0-2 years.......................................16-17
    2-5 years..20
    5-12 years...23
    12-18 years......................................25-6
soft drinks...10, 69-70
solid foods...16
soy milk..55, 68
sports..12, 24, 27
strength/resistance activities..........................83
stress...102
sugar..5, 10
    hidden...56
sweets...56

T

tantrums..22, 43
teenagers............................25-7, 84, 92
    dieting...35
teething..19
television...........................11, 37, 84, 102
toddlers.............................16-19, 32, 83
tooth decay...70-1

U

Use By date...79

V

variety, in food...57
vegetable juice...69
vegetables..10, 17, 33
    food group..52
vegetarian diets.....................................54, 114
video games..................................24, 102
vitamins...74

W

walking...85, 86
water..66-7
weight gain..22, 33
    poor, in infancy...................................18
weight loss..35
weight problems..........................5, 10, 13
    recognising.......................................30-1
work, part-time, effect on exercise...................27

Published in 2007 by Murdoch Books Pty Limited

www.murdochbooks.com.au

Murdoch Books Australia
Pier 8/9, 23 Hickson Road, Millers Point NSW 2000
Phone: +61 (0) 2 8220 2000 Fax: +61 (0) 2 8220 2558

Murdoch Books UK Limited
Erico House, 6th Floor North, 93–99 Upper Richmond Road,
Putney, London SW15 2TG
Phone: +44 (0) 20 8785 5995 Fax: +44 (0) 20 8785 5985

Chief Executive: Juliet Rogers
Publishing Director: Kay Scarlett
Graphic Design and Illustrations: Lisa Danilko

Printed by Midas Printing (Asia) Ltd in 2007. Printed in China.

Text © 2007 Berry Ernest Publishing

Stock images courtesy of Shutterstock.com and iStockphoto.com

National Library of Australia Cataloguing-in-Publication Data

Mason, Phillip

abc Guide to Fit Kids: a companion for parents and families.
ISBN 978 1 92125 948 7 (pbk).
ISBN 1 92125 948 5 (pbk).
1. Children – Health and hygiene. 2. Children – Nutrition.
3. Exercise for children. 4. Child development. I. Swan,
Katherine. II. Stone, Adrian. III. Title.
613.7042

A CIP catalogue record for this book is available from the British Library

Visit www.abcfitkids.com for more information, parent's blog,
free downloadable fact sheets, resources and recipes.